Author: D. Fred Murray
Editor: Jody L. Murray

God Loves Even Cowboys

Murray Publishing, Box 99-A, Firth, NE 68358

Cover drawing used by permission of the artist, Kim McGinness

Library of Congress Cataloging-in-Publication Number 94-096344

ISBN: 0-9642685-4-X

First Edition printing Aug. 1994.

Printed in the U.S.A.

Dedication

To the ladies in my life who inspire me the most:

My Wife, Mary Ann
My Sister, Mary Ellen
My Mother, Luella

And to my friend, Lula, who patiently
worked with and inspired me.

CHAPTERS

God Loves Even Cowboys

Introduction

Come along with me. I have saddled a gentle old mare for you to ride. We will ride the story trails of this book. We will also take a look at the scenery of the Old West as we travel.

May you enjoy reading these stories as much as I do, telling and drawing them. I do not intend for them to be historical facts. Dates and geography are purposely left out because it is cow country lore. Historical records may shed some different light, but here is how I came about the stories that I did not witness.

When I was a very small child, and growing up, I remember on cold days sitting at the south side of a building or a hay stack in the sun, listening to the old time cowboys discuss past time and events. I soon learned to be seen and not heard, and in doing so, I was filled with many stories and events of the Old West.

I cannot remember a time when we were not holding a cattle shipment on the train. This was before we had large trucks to haul them. There were large ranches and many little ranches pooled together that stayed at our ranch overnight or until they could get a train car to load their cattle on.

It was an exciting time, wild cattle, cowboys and a lot of good saddle horses. I knew who would be coming and when they would arrive. At school, I would use the excuse of needing to go to the restroom, then would leave for home, with my good "Ole" mustang cow pony, Peaches. I would be at the edge of our valley in time to help them through the lanes to our ranch. By the age of seven, I could handle the winter feed rack with a gentle team of horses, so that by summer, I could get a job driving stacker horses in the hay fields.

Cow country and all that is involved, horses, cattle, people and the range, have always held a great fascination for me. Growing up on a ranch in cow country and working there until I got married, gave me the knowledge, as well as the craft of the trade. The memories of these, and other cattle drives, along with cow camps, roundup and brandings, is where I have gotten my large number of stories.

I want to thank those closest to me who were my capable teachers. First and foremost my father, Ivan Murray, also Pap Finley, Bob, John and Russ Latham, Warren Paddock, Carl and Delos Webb, Bill Hahn and those other old time cattlemen too numerous to mention.

Special Thanks to Lula Masters, whose faith, persistence and hard work inspired me to start this project. Lula spent hours recording me telling the stories contained in this book. Then Lula with the help of Debbie Whitson typed the stories just as I had told them.

My son Joe along with our good friend Camille Wolezensky spent hundreds of hours assisting me in organizing, editing and proofreading. Thank You very much for your hard work and dedication.

My daughter-in-Law Sharon and my wife Mary Ann provided invaluable assistance in proofreading. Most importantly they patiently gave me the love and support needed to finish this project.

Frosty Nesmith helped bring this old cowboy into the modern age of technology by providing advice and assistance about computers. He made it possible for my simple drawings to be in this book.

Finally, I must pay special tribute to Kim McGinness for allowing me to share with you her extraordinary talent. Kim your talent speaks for itself, but I am still amazed that you can even make an old cowboy like me look good.

Fred has been an inspiration to me for many years. As I sat with a group of young people around a campfire listening to his stories, the Lord impressed upon me that we needed to put these stories in a book.

Thanks Fred for the privilege and the honor of helping in this small way, to get these stories made into a book. My prayer is that each heart will know Jesus better after reading these stories.

Lula Masters

CAUGHT IN A BLIZZARD

"Dad tied ole Dick down then covered with saddle, blanket and pad."

As Sky helped his sister Merle tuck the younger children into bed, he wondered whether he would ever see any of them again for tonight was the night Sky planned to leave home. Sky went to his room as he normally did at bed time and got in bed, but he didn't take his clothes off. He lay there waiting for the clock to strike ten. By then, he knew everyone would be asleep including his father.

Sky wasn't this twelve year old boy's real name. His mother named him Nelson Ivan Murray and as was the tradition in the Murray family he was to go by his middle name. However when he was seven, Ivan took a fancy to a big beautiful buckskin mustang that his father ran in off the range. Ivan pleaded with his father to let him have this horse. His father said, "Well kid if you think you're man enough to have a horse then you can earn it just like any other man. You have to break him." His father snubbed the bronc colt up against another horse and saddled him. Then Ivan got on and his father turned the bronc loose. The horse exploded in every direction, twisting and turning. The horse proved to be too much for a seven year old boy and it sent Ivan flying. Ivan's father laughed at him and started calling him Sky because the horse had thrown him "sky high." Ivan resented it, but the name stuck with his family.

As he lie there waiting for the clock to strike ten, Sky thought back over the events that led up to his decision to run away from home. His mother died when he was eight and it became the responsibility of his sister Merle and himself to take care of the younger children. Furthermore Sky took on most of the responsibility of running the ranch because his father worked for sheriff Pope as a deputy and spent a lot of time away from home chasing outlaws. When he wasn't on the trail of an outlaw, he was usually at the local saloon playing cards or carousing with some woman. Sky had to quit school to do the ranch work and take care of the children. When his father was home he spent his time giving orders for the work that he expected Sky to do or punishing him because he hadn't done something the way that he told him to do it.

Sky's father had 3,000 sheep and 500 head of cattle. In the winter he brought them off the open range and kept them in fenced yards where he fed them hay. Many times he purposely opened the gate and let them out. Then he made Sky go get them back in the field before he could have supper or go to bed. If he didn't, he would get a beating, I don't mean a licking, I mean a beating.

Eventually Sky figured out what his father was doing so he didn't get them in one day. His father was furious with him and gave him an extra hard beating. After this, Sky decided he couldn't take much more of this so he started thinking about running away from home. A few days later, his father announced he was getting married again.

This was the final straw for Sky so he started planning how to get away. Sky had an old black horse named Dick that his uncle had given him. He decided that some night he would sneak out of the house, get on Dick and leave the country. There was one problem with his plan and that was the dog. If he went out the dog would bark and alert his father. Every night for several weeks, he sneaked a biscuit or piece of meat from the table. After everyone was sleeping, he opened the window and fed the dog so that the dog wouldn't bark when he left.

When the clock struck ten, it was time to put his plan into effect. He got up and put a few extra clothes into a gunny sack. He raised the window and the dog came for his food. While the dog was eating, Sky crawled out the window and went to the barn. His horse was ready to go because he had saddled him when he did the evening chores. He led him a mile and a half. The dog didn't bark or follow.

It was an unusually warm evening for early April as Sky mounted Dick and put him into a slow lope. There were a few clouds to the Northwest above the Unitah Mountains, but Sky didn't give them any thought because he was thinking only of his new found freedom. He headed East toward the K Ranch, which was on the Colorado and Utah border about 40-45 miles away. Early the next morning just before sunrise a spring blizzard came up. The wind was blowing so hard and it was snowing so heavy that he couldn't see were he was going and had no way to build a fire. He knew he needed protection from the storm, so he put a rope around the horse's feet and jerked his feet out from under him. He then tied all four feet together, took his saddle blanket and saddle off his back and then lay between the horse's belly, feet and legs, covering himself with the blanket and saddle.

It wasn't long before the snow covered them up. Sky went to sleep nice and warm in his snug bed with the snow on top and snuggled by the warm body of the horse. Sometime later, the horse began to move, which woke Sky. He dug himself out of the snow and saw that it was clear as a bell. He was on top of a ridge. He looked down in the valley and within a mile was the K Ranch. It was the middle of the morning, so he untied his horse and got him up. Sky came through the storm just fine, but "Ole" Dick didn't fair so well. He was about dead. Both his tail and ears were frozen off.

"Dad shore had a fine outfit." That's all he had left after three years work.

Bart Lewis, the manager of the K ranch, was a friend of Sky's father. They played cards and drank together. Therefore Sky didn't want to stop at the ranch, but with the condition Dick was in he had no choice. When Sky got to the ranch, Bart said, "What are you doing here." Sky told him that he was pulling out, in other words, leaving home. Bart said, "Well as soon as breakfast is over, I'm taking you back to your old man and he can tan your hide for trying to be smart like that." However, Bart didn't reckon with this 12 year old boy. This boy had been working and was a seasoned man. He wasn't like other 12 year old boys.

After Sky finished eating, they went to the barn where Bart told Sky, "All right, you saddle that horse." So Sky threw his saddle on a K Ranch horse. Sky pulled the gun out of the scabbard on his saddle and put a shell in the chamber. When Bart turned around, he was facing the gun barrel of the big rifle. Sky told Bart, "There's one thing; you can try to take me back, but I'm going to kill you if you do." Bart changed his mind very fast and decided the best thing to do was to give Sky a job. Bart outfitted Sky with a string of horses and a camp outfit and took him up to Blue Mountain to catch wild horses. Bart was looking out for his health when he made this decision, but he also knew Sky was a good hand for his age because of the work his father made him do.

Sky was up there three years and Bart Lewis was the only one who knew where he was. A couple of times a year he'd bring Sky some bacon, a bottle of whiskey, new Levis, a new shirt and maybe a new pair of boots. Sky got $15 a month for catching wild horses. The average pay then for a regular cowboy was $10.

Although Sky knew a lot more about horses and ranching than most boys his age let alone some men, there were numerous things he had to learn on his own. He built a corral, dug a trench and cut the cedar posts and stuck them in the ground. They were about 12-15 feet high so the horses couldn't jump over them and the corral tapered round, leaning to the outside. If you were riding a horse in the corral, he couldn't get your leg up against the fence. On this particular corral he built two long walls or fences running out from the corral to the head of the canyon. He would shove the horses off into this canyon where he had built a fence across the other opening. Once he had them in the canyon, he could put the bars up and they couldn't leave the canyon. There was water and feed for them. He ran them in whenever he wanted until he had them all broke. Once they were all broke, he shoved out the gate on the lower end of the canyon, which led down to the ranch. When these horses got to the ranch nobody knew who was catching and breaking them except for Bart and Sky.

Three years went by and Sky now 15 years old thought he was big and tough. I suppose he was, because how many 15 year old boys could catch, break and ride wild horses by themselves. He had done a good job of it and broke many good horses. He rode by the ranch and drew his pay. Then he rode back to town 40 miles away with his few belongings tied in a sack. He stopped by the saddle shop and the hardware store where he bought himself a tent, camping equipment, skillets and cooking utensils, a good warm bed roll, some new clothes, a new pair of boots, a new saddle and bridle. He had his own horses because he had caught some horses and brought them with him. Now he was ready to see his old man.

Since I mentioned that his father was a deputy sheriff, maybe we better back up a little bit to the morning Sky pulled out. When Sky's father realized that he was gone and that he'd taken a horse, it made him so angry he went down and had the man at the newspaper print up a "wanted dead or alive" poster for horse thief on his own son. He went all over putting up the posters.

Back then you had men, called bounty hunters, who were cowards. They would shoot anybody if they were wanted whether they had committed a crime or not. They would generally wait around and shoot a man in the back. When it said dead or alive, they'd shoot the man, tie him across the back of a horse and they got $100 plus the horse. This was a business for these killers.

When Uncle Jerry, the one who had given this old black horse to Sky, saw one of the posters; he went in and laid it on the father's desk, saying, "Now Hatch, whatever shape the boy's brought in, that's the shape I'm going to bring you in." In other words, if they had killed Sky, that's what Uncle Jerry was going to do to his own brother.

When Sky's father was an old, old man in the nursing home, he still laughed about ruining and wearing out a good horse picking up all the posters before a bounty hunter found them.

When Sky, or I should say Ivan as he was now called, got back out to the ranch, his father wasn't there because he was at the sheriff's office, but his new wife was there. She was very ill lying in bed. Ivan asked her, "Have you seen the doctor?"

She said, "No, your father says it's cheaper to let me die than to get the doctor." Sky went out to the barn, caught a team of horses, hooked them to the spring wagon and put some hay in the back of the wagon. He laid a mattress on it and carried this lady out to the wagon. He took her to the hotel in town, went down the street, got the doctor and took him to the hotel. He took all the money he had left from his three years' wages and gave it to the doctor and hotel keeper. He laid it on the table and said, "You see that this woman gets all the medical care she needs and if the money runs out before that, let me know and I'll pay you the rest."

Ivan wasn't a church goer but he had very good Christian qualities and to the very day Aunt Ziny died, she would hug him and say, "I love this man more than anybody because he saved my life."

Ivan decided he didn't want to go back to the mountain to run wild horses because it was a very hard way to make a living. His father talked Sky into herding sheep. He told Ivan, "We're going to take the sheep to Colorado, over by Aspen, they'll summer there, then in the winter we'll bring them back to the desert and you'll get half of the lamb crop and half of the wool crop." Despite his father's past actions, Ivan wanted to believe his father so he agreed to the deal.

About the middle of the summer a man came to camp with three Mexican herders. Ivan was eating breakfast and the man said, "Hit the trail." The man produced a paper saying that he owned all the sheep and the whole outfit. Ivan's father had been in a poker game a few nights before, losing the sheep and all of his cattle.

So Ivan said, "Why don't you boys sit down and eat, I'll leave after I get done eating." Now, understanding the man's treachery, Ivan went to get something and when he did he grabbed his rifle, turned around with it loaded and cocked. He backed the man and the sheepherders away from him. They were all scared. While Ivan held the gun on them, he made one of the sheepherders take down the tent, catch the pack horses that were Ivan's personal horses, and gather Ivan's personal things. The man was protesting. "I got all of that."

Ivan said, "No you didn't, these are my personal things, you'll have to settle with my old man." When everything was loaded, he got on his horse and drove them way away from where their horses were, spooked the horses so the men couldn't get a gun and chase him. He'd worked about a year and a half for nothing.

After that, he worked for the Two Bars and the K Ranch. Ivan who was my father was a very good cowboy and drew top wages because he could do anything.

We shouldn't let our problems affect us. My father Ivan was always cheerful and he was always happy. He took care of my grandfather when he was an old man and he was kind to him, he never held a grudge.

OLD BILL PATTON

Leavin for work. "About sunup these ole ponies shore felt good."

Bill came to the western slope to run the Two Bars Cattle Company. Bill was a man that you could say was not all good or not all bad. He was a very good cowman when and if he wanted to be. He was very knowledgeable about horses, cattle and the men that handled them. At that time, Two Bars had about 68,000 head of cattle on the western slope and 150,000 on the Laramie Plains. In those days, they used roundup wagons. The Two Bars had 9 of them with about 25 men and from 5 to 10 reps. It was all open range for 150 miles in every direction and there were no fences. The reps were from other ranches and could pick their cattle out of the larger herds of the Two Bars. My father had just quit my grandfather's sheep operation and had gone back to Blue Mountain to run wild horses. Bill sent word to the McNurlen camp that he needed them for roundup so my father was one of the men Guy McNurlen asked to come and work as a rep at the Two Bars.

At first, things went along fairly smooth between Bill and Father. However when the roundup was into its second month, Old Bill began to pick on Dad. He was never satisfied with anything Dad did, cussing him out in front of the men morning and night. He criticized everything that Dad did. Guy and Bobby Bowen, the cook, told Dad that if he wanted, they would help him get even with Old Patton. They put together a plan, but to put it in effect they would need a dozen cockleburs.

Bill always kept the horse he used on a picket rope instead of with the herd like the other men. He always got up with the cook and sent the nighthawk for the horses. As soon as the nighthawk left to bring in the cavvy, he saddled his horse and ate breakfast. By the time the horse herd was corralled, he was ready to go for the day though it was not yet time to start. That was his way to be mean. By being the first one ready, he would cuss and hurry the men to leave camp. He kept the insults flying until everyone mounted. Then he would be the last one to mount his horse.

This particular morning, he was more offensive than ever. Dad and Guy got ready to go just a little sooner than the other cowboys. They moved around close to Bill's horse after he was saddled and put the cockleburs under that poor pony's saddle blanket. Everyone was mounted and ready to go except Bill, because Bobby kept talking to delay him. Dad and Guy didn't mount either but stayed on the ground so they could hold their horses. Well, when Bill sat down in his saddle, that colt felt those burrs, bogged his head and really went to bucking!

The range horse was a strange sort of creature, if one bucked, they would all buck just as hard as the one who had started it. When they started to buck, some went right through the remuda and those horses that had run wild in this area, struck out for the home range. When the fracas was over, there were only three riders who had stayed with their horses. It took three days to catch enough horses to mount half the cowboys. There were three saddles that never got caught until the fall roundup five months later.

It didn't take long for Old Bill and four of his cronies to figure out who had a part in the fracas. They grabbed Dad and stretched him face down across the back of a gentle horse and started to beat him with a pair of chaps. Bobby Bowen, the cook, grabbed his meat cleaver, which was sharp enough to chop steak and bone all with one chop, ran to where they were beating the cowboy and told Bill, "If you hit the kid again you will lose your head."

At the same time, Guy McNurlen stuck a loaded and cocked 30/30 rifle barrel against Bill's left ear and said, "Hit him once more and your brain will be scattered to the wind."

However before those few hard blows stopped, my father was badly hurt. Bobby made him a bed in the wagon and cared for him as if he was a small child. It was five days before Dad was up and moving again. Old Bill was always afraid to even speak to Dad because he knew Bobby and Guy were just looking for an excuse!

It wasn't long because of Bill's poor management and shady dealings that the owner had to sell the western slope cattle and horses as well as the deeded land.

I often think of this man when I see selfish and thoughtless people. They all seem to come to the same kind of an end. There is an old saying that goes something like this, "What goes around comes around".

NO ONE EVER EATS MY BEEF

"We hung the hide inside the cabin."

I always laugh at the story my father told about representing one of the ranches at a roundup. Representatives, called "reps" were cowboys who would go on roundups to look for cattle on another ranch's range. They would take their own string of horses and bedding with them to the roundup and would work for the other ranch's foreman following his instructions. When the roundup was over and the cattle separated, a "rep" would take his ranch's cattle with him.

Dad's boss sent him to "rep" for his outfit at the K-T Ranch spring roundup. The owner, a man who liked to brag on himself, always ran the roundup. The thing that irritated the cowboys the most was that he thought he was so tough that everyone was afraid of him. At meal time, he bragged that no one ever rustled or ate his beef. When the roundup was over, my father and another rep were going about 60 miles in the same direction. After traveling most of the day, they came to one of the K-T's cow camps. While there, they saw a steer with the K-T's brand. Being young men with daring spirits, they thought it would be fun to kill and butcher this steer. They hung the hide on the ridgepole inside the cabin, so when you walked in the door, the K-T brand would be the first thing seen. They put the beef from the steer on their pack horses and gave it to the homesteaders they passed as they travelled through the country.

My dad and the other rep he travelled with in the spring were both sent back to the K-T to rep the fall roundup. The owner never said a word about how no one ate his beef. Accidentally, one cowboy brought up the subject of killing and eating someone else's beef. The owner got very angry and made a long speech about people going through the country killing other people's beef. Dad and Harry gave each other a knowing look.

Be very careful about bragging, because it can come back to haunt you.

400 DOLLAR RIDE

Four Hundred Dollars. "I stuck my spur in his shoulder joint." "That ole Ute pony never bucked again."

The early days of rodeo were a lot different from the way it is today with its large arenas and bucking chutes. The early rodeos consisted mostly of saddle bronc riding and roping cattle. The rodeo began as a way to settle a dispute between two ranches over whose cowboys were the better riders and ropers. The two ranches would get together for a 3 day event to settle the dispute. For the first day and a half they rode broncs. Then they competed in roping events for the last day and a half. It proved to be great fun for both the participants and spectators.

Out on the range, a cowboy had to ride a bucking horse until it stopped. He might get himself busted up and stranded as much as 100 miles away from a town or settlement. If you were a wild horse breaker like my father, you might be that far from the nearest person because you had to go where the mustangs were and they were as far away from people as they could get. For this reason, the early rodeo's didn't just expect you to ride the bronc for a few seconds; you rode the horse until he stopped bucking. After all, the purpose of riding a horse was to gentle him so he could be useful in handling cattle or at the least to provide dependable transportation.

Instead of having a fancy chute where the cowboy can get set just right before the gate opened and the horse started bucking, the old-timers would pull the head of the bronc over the back of another horse while the cowboy saddled the bronc. Then, the cowboy would swing on and they turned the bronc loose. Sometimes they were in a corral, but often they were out in the open. The riding could take a few seconds or all day, depending on the skill and endurance of the cowboy and the determination of the bronc he was riding to resist being controlled.

This type of rodeo led to the big sport it is today. Now the rodeo cowboy is an athlete just like a football or basketball player. They go to schools that teach them how to perform and have conditioning programs just like any other athlete. However most of these "cowboys" couldn't get a cow out of the brush or ride a bucking horse outside the rodeo arena if their life depended on it. Furthermore it was a display of the cowboy's skills used every day to make a living out on the open range. His talent came from hard work and necessity. He could not survive if he didn't learn to ride and rope well. The original rodeo was a celebration of being good at what you do for a living.

There was one particular horse that belonged to some Indians that no one seemed to be able to handle. He threw everyone that dared trying to ride him. At every rodeo several cowboys would put $25 in a pool and the cowboy that could stay on that horse would win the pool. The $25 fee was over a month's pay, so it put a big hole in the pocket of those cowboys who had the bad luck trying to stay on that ornery bronc.

My father studied that ornery bronc every time the bronc sent the latest cowboy flying along with his 25 bucks. Dad memorized every twist and turn the bronc made until he thought he figured out how to ride him. When the pool reached $400, Dad decided the time was right to risk investing his $25.

Before going to put his money down, Dad sharpened his spurs so that if the horse was tougher than he thought, he could then work him over with the spurs. Nobody noticed his spurs when Dad put his money down. Well, they snubbed that bronc up tight over the back of another horse while Dad was putting on his rigging. Dad swung on and they turned the bronc loose. That bronc erupted with the force of a volcano. It turned and twisted in every direction hitting the ground with the force of a pile driver. Dad immediately realized that this bronc was a lot tougher than he had figured. To try to stay on and wear the horse down, Dad stuck his razor sharp spurs in that ornery bronc's shoulders. The spur happened to catch right in the shoulder joint injuring the bronc, causing him to fall and stay down. The rules said that to win the rider must stay on until the horse stopped bucking. Since Dad stayed on until it stopped bucking, he went to claim the prize. However, the Indians didn't see it that way. They argued that since Dad injured the horse, he shouldn't collect. As sheriff of the county, Grandfater judged the event. He sided with Dad, ruling that Dad had ridden the horse until he stopped bucking, which entitled Dad to the $400. Thus, Dad walked away with almost two years' wages for just a few seconds' work.

Remember this, if you want something bad enough do not listen to the nay sayers who say you can't accomplish your goal. If you keep working hard to achieve your goal, you can accomplish it even though you might experience many set backs and disappointments along the way. If your goal is good and just, you have the most powerful force in the universe at your disposal to help you succeed. All you have to do is ask Jesus to help and He will. "Ask and it shall be given unto you."

ROPING A BEAR

"Dad finally got her cut loose."

To be a good roper, you had to practice all the time. The old time cowboys loved to rope and they roped many things. Roping was an essential part of their job. For practice and to have a little fun, they would rope some wild animal. One of their favorites was a coyote. After roping the coyote they shot him so they could get the rope off.

One time my father and another cowboy roped a bear. With something as large and mean as a bear it took two of them to be able to stretch the bear out and shoot him so they could get their rope back.

One day while riding alone, Father saw this yearling black bear eating berries in the bushes. Father spooked it out of the bushes and got it running. Then he took down his rope. He was a good roper and caught the bear. After he caught the bear, Father realized he didn't know how he was going to get his rope off. He didn't have his gun with him and didn't want to lose his rope.

While he was trying to figure this out, the bear was getting angry, which was scaring his horse. That bear was pretty smart. He figured out that he couldn't get loose by fighting the rope so the bear twisted its paws around the rope and started climbing the rope. The bear was almost on top of them and the horse was bucking and running in an attempt to get away. Father was trying to stay on the horse, while attempting to get his knife out of his pocket, which was covered by his chaps. At the same time he was kicking and pushing the bear away with his foot.

Finally he got his pocket knife out and cut the rope. When he was loose, the bear took off. This incident completely ruined the horse as a roping horse because every time someone took a rope down, the horse would always stop and start to tremble.

Sometimes the devil gets a rope on us, entangling us in such a way that we think we can never get free. When this happens, the Lord is always there to cut us loose if we just ask him.

CATCHING THE OLD BUCKSKIN

"One rope tied to a tree, one tied fast to saddle." "As he came out of the draw, I got the tree loop on him."

After the celebration and rodeo on the 4th of July, the cowboys who weren't needed on the big cattle drives would be laid off until fall roundup. Those laid off ran wild horses. They went out in the hills and chased the mustangs until they caught them or ran them into traps. Then they broke them to ride and sold them for $10 to $15 a head. Since this was as much as they were getting paid by the ranches for a whole months work, it made for a profitable venture.

Down on the desert, on the Colorado and Utah line, west of

Rangely, Colorado, there was this herd of wild mustangs led by an old buckskin stud. He was the only wild stud that my father or any of the old wild horse runners ever saw leading a band of wild horses. Generally an old mare called the "lead mare" would lead the herd with the stallion coming behind driving and protecting his band. However, this old buckskin was always in the lead. He tolerated another young horse to go behind driving the herd.

In the past, many cowboys tried to catch that old stud without success. My father and two of his friends decided that when they were laid off after the 4th of July, they would go down and see if they could catch this old buckskin horse.

They quickly found the buckskin's band, but things went down hill from there. When the mustangs saw them, they took off as hard as they could go. The three men tried to cut them off and turn them toward one of the traps they had built. As they tried to cut them off, one cowboy's horse stumbled and fell. The horse and cowboy rolled over right into the cactus. The other two helped the cowboy out of the cactus and took him back to camp where they worked well into the night taking all the little stickers out. If they didn't get them all out they would become infected and the cowboy would get very sick.

The next day, they went out and the second fella's horse fell in a gully and rolled him into the cactus. Again, they spent most of that night by the campfire picking out stickers.

Well, after the fate of his two friends my father was getting mighty superstitious. The next morning Father decided that it might be his turn to take a roll in the cactus, so he decided to stay in camp. Father made an excuse to his friends that he needed to fix his saddle so he stayed in camp while the other two went out to chase the buckskin.

The camp was near the top of a big ridge under a cliff, which gave Dad a view of the whole country for 10 to 15 miles in every direction. He could see the chase start because of the cloud of dust made by the running band of mustangs. The cowboys' horses couldn't run as fast as this old stallion and his band. Suddenly the cloud of dust disappeared.

Dad figured the mustang band had to go one of two directions. They would hit this big gully and would have to go down toward the Green River, which would be a dead end unless they swam the river to get out of the gully or they could go to a large flat with some juniper trees where they could hide.

Deciding that the junipers would be where they would head rather than swimming the river, Dad saddled his horse, grabbed an extra lariat and rode the four miles from camp as hard as his horse could go. When he got there he could hear them coming up the gully.

The ole Outlaw. "That ole Buckskin shore brokeout." He was shore a pile driver."

Dad took a sixty foot lariat and tied one end to a cedar tree. When the old buckskin stud came out of the gully, Dad roped him with the rope tied to the tree. He then took his forty foot rope from the saddle and roped the horse again. When done, Dad stretched the horse out between the tree and his saddle horse.

Dad took his gun out of his scabbard and shot in the air to get the other cowboys' attention. When they arrived, they took their ropes and jerked the old buckskin's feet out from under him, hog-tying and saddling the horse. He gave Dad a real "run for his money" when they turned him loose. Eventually he was broke to ride and over time became a good horse. By checking his teeth, they figured he was 12-14 years old when they caught him.

One time Dad was 100 miles from home, when he received word that his stepmother was very ill. He saddled up the old buckskin and started for home. About half way there, his pack horse gave out so he left him at a ranch and continued on. Dad and the old buckskin made the 100 miles all in one day, which is a tremendous amount of miles for one horse to go in a day. The buckskin's feet, ankles and joints swelled so much that he could barely move for three days and he was so tired he couldn't eat. After a week or so, he fully recovered.

That buckskin was a very faithful old horse so Dad gave him to Uncle Jerry, the man that saved Dad when his father put out the wanted posters on Dad for "stealing" his own horse. They figured the old horse was over 30 when he died. Uncle Jerry used him to herd sheep for at least 12 years.

You know, sometimes we look at people and they are rough looking but maybe if we really got to know them, they would be kind and gentle like the old buckskin mustang.

HORSE IN DISPUTE

"No one ever seen him again." I was the only one that knew where he was buried.

This story was not told to me this way. I pieced it together. In other words, little pieces of the story were told to me at different times and eventually the whole story of what happened came together.

Dad was about 17 years old and was up on Blue Mountain catching wild horses for Bart Lewis of the K Ranch. They shipped some of the horses east, sold some to other ranchers and the rest they used on the K Ranch.

One of the men Dad worked with, Bart hired when he went to Cheyenne Frontier Days. The fellow who had won the top saddle bronc riding event met Bart and asked him for a job as he wanted to quit rodeoing. He said he was a good bronc rider so Bart hired him. Eventually he wound up on the mountain at Dad's camp. Dad said as long as the man was in a pen or a corral, he could really ride a horse. "You just stood in awe at how good he could ride." When he went through the open gate, things changed. There were rocks, cactus, rattle snakes, holes, trees and brush all of which scared this man. He would fall off the same horse that he had no problem riding in the corral. This went along for about 2 weeks. Every time they went out of the corral, the man got bucked off and Dad had to chase down the fella's saddle. Then the guy would ride him in the pen.

They camped out in the hills by a spring where they had a wild horse trap. When Dad got up one morning, the fella had Dad's personal horse saddled. Dad said to him, "Where are you going?"

The man replied, "I'm leaving."

"You're not leaving with my horse!" Dad snapped back as he pulled his rifle on the man. That's where Dad quit telling the story. I asked him one time if anyone ever saw the fella again? He said, "Nope, nope, nobody ever saw him again."

Time went on and he told me the story several times but would always stop in the same place. It was as if he wanted to tell me more, but he just couldn't do it.

When he was an old man, just before he died, he said to my mother, "I should go back to Blue Mountain because I know where a man is buried. I'm the only one who knows the story of what happened and I'm the only one who knows where he's buried." The next time I saw Dad, I asked him about this story. He did not come right out and say that he had killed the man, but he came so close that I knew that's what happened. The man was going to leave on Dad's horse so Dad shot him. In those days, it was legal, because he was stealing Dad's personal horse.

For over 50 years Dad carried this guilt in his soul. Before he died, he had to make it right with somebody. The only person he could tell was my mother.

Friends, it doesn't pay to hide our guilt. We are responsible for the things we do. We must confess and God will cleanse us and bring us happiness.

TOO BUSTED TO MOVE

Broken leg. "That ole pony stumble and fell over the rim."

When my father was about 16, he was out in the hills by himself running wild horses. Cowboys don't worry about how steep the mountain is; they just put their spurs to their horse and down they go. Dad was coming around the side of the mountain going like the wind, chasing and trying to cut some horses off and head them toward his trap, when his horse slipped and fell. They were on the steep side of a mountain and the horse started to slide. Soon they came to a rim rock with a twenty foot drop and down over the rim rock they went. The horse landed on top of Dad and they slid to the bottom of the hill by a creek.

The horse got up, but when Dad tried to get up, he couldn't because right below his left knee, both bones were broken. There he sat; he couldn't get on his horse, because all horses were broke to be mounted on the left side. Most horses would not even let a cowboy get close to the right side.

Broken leg. "To busted to move."

Dad took his 40 foot lariat rope and tied his horse to a tree and pulled the saddle off. He thought, "In a day or two I'll fix me a splint and I'll then be able to get back on the horse some way and we'll ride home." It was six weeks before he finally got back on the horse. During those six weeks, he and his horse almost starved to death.

It was only about a three hour ride back to camp, but no one knew where Dad was. He had no food or bed roll so he rolled up in his saddle blanket. His leg hurt him badly, but he did the best he could to straighten it out. He got some sticks of wood and cut some string from his saddle, lacing the leg to the sticks, which made kind of a splint. He had no choice, but to wait until the leg healed enough he could get on the bronc.

After about a week, he was getting mighty hungry so he shot a jack rabbit. He dragged himself to the rabbit and back to the fire by his camp. A cowboy camp was wherever he had a fire, water and his bedroll. He roasted the rabbit the best he could and rationed it out over several days, but it didn't last long. He caught a horny toad that came by and held him over the fire until he had roasted the toad. In time, he was able to catch a little 6 inch long fish that he roasted and ate. During the six weeks that was all he had to eat.

Broken leg. "Grub was gettin mighty short."

During this time, the horse ate all the grass and vegetation he could reach. He stood on his hind legs and reached as high as he could in the trees. He was so hungry he chewed on the wood of the trees. He had already ate the bark off.

Dad was afraid to let the horse go because he might get away. After six weeks his leg healed enough that he could stand on it, but he was so weak he could hardly get the saddle on his horse. It took him about three hours. He hobbled back and forth to get the cinch tight enough, as the horse was so thin.

Finally, Dad got in the saddle and let the horse graze. He just kept grazing. Dad never got off until they arrived at camp three days later. It usually only took three hours.

No matter what our situation is, and no matter how bad it looks, God always looks out for us. My father was very fortunate because God let him land near wood so he could have a warm fire at night and by a stream of water so he would have water to drink.

JERKED DOWN

"Poor ole Ross was left a cripple for the rest of his life."

Logan Mountain is one of those long ridges that sticks out in the oil shale plateau of northwestern Colorado and is where this story begins. I guess I was probably six years old when this story took place. It was the first flashlight I'd ever seen and it made a deep impression on my mind. I didn't understand the true importance of what really happened that terrible day up on the top of Logan Mountain until I grew up.

It was supper time when two men rode up to our house. It was Ralph who was a big, good cow man and the doctor. They asked my father if he would go with them to bring a man off Logan Mountain. As a child I was taught to be seen and not heard, so when they came, I got as close as I could to hear the conversation, but yet not be a part of it. Earlier that day, a man roped a big steer and the steer got sideways to his horse, pulling the man down. The rope tangled around the horse causing the man to be tied up in the saddle and the steer drug the horse across the man several times. Finally, someone shot the steer, cut the rope and got the horse off the man whose name was Ross. He was badly injured with his spine, hips, legs and ribs broken. He was more dead than alive.

Ross was hurt at about 10:00 in the morning. It was about 6:00 in the evening when Ralph and the doctor came to get my father. This happened many years ago when we didn't have fancy Ford or Chevy pickups and the roads were not paved. Highway 6, which is now an interstate through western Colorado was just a dirt and gravel road.

They had a Model A pickup. They put some hay and a mattress in the back of the pickup, which was the ambulance for bringing Ross back. They drove the 15 or 20 miles to the end of the trail, where they parked the pickup and walked 15 miles to where they found Ross lying in the sagebrush. When they got there, it was late and there was no moon, but they were able to find him because there was a big campfire with eight or ten people sitting around it, fortifying themselves with a bottle. Not one of them was helping poor Ross.

Dad, Ralph and the doctor could see that Ross was badly broken. Dad asked if they had an axe at the cow camp. Ralph went down, got the axe and found two strong Aspen poles just the right size for holding on to. They gathered up saddle blankets, lariats and chaps with which to make a stretcher. Between the doctor, Ralph and Father, they gently moved him over onto the stretcher. Ross was barely conscious, but he did recognize them.

The other people, some of them were members of his family, had just been sitting there not willing to walk that steep trail at night. If my father, Ross and the doctor had not come, they would have waited until daylight, swung Ross between two horses on a stretcher tied on poles across the saddles with a man leading both horses. My father, Ralph and the doctor knew that if they didn't get Ross to the hospital he would soon be dead.

Doc walked along, holding the flashlight, while Ralph and Father carried the stretcher. This is how they began their 15 mile trip back to the pickup. When they got so tired their arms ached, they squatted down, resting the end of the poles of the homemade stretcher on their knees. They sat in a squatting position because they did not want him to touch the ground again because he was in terrible pain.

At last they reached the pickup. They laid him on the mattress in the hay, which made a fairly soft bed. Dad sat on one side of the pickup and Doc sat on the other. They held a large tarp over Ross to protect him from the wind, while Ralph drove the 60 miles to the hospital. The Model A pickup went 30 m.p.h. at top speed if the road would allow it. By morning they finally reached Glenwood Springs.

Over time, Ross healed, but it left him very crippled. He was happy to be able to just walk around. His right leg was always crooked and twisted. Even though he hobbled, he was very optimistic, as most old western cowboys were. After all, he was still alive and getting hurt was just part of life. He was a ranch owner and life was good to him. An old western cowboy rarely complained. I can remember going to cow camp, seeing him with his old gentle horse. He would lead the horse up to a rock or a wagon tongue and to put it in his words, "I would waller on."

I remember the first time I went to cow camp. Ross would come to cow camp and help drive the cows. He was the cook and was very good. The first thing he always did was to tell me how great my daddy was. He'd say, "My own family, my own cousin wouldn't carry me in that night. Your daddy, Ralph and Doc saved my life."

The old time cowboy was a jovial, happy person. He was optimistic and loved to play jokes. That first morning at camp we sat down at the table. Of course, I thought I was lucky, I wasn't near home or my mother, so they poured me a cup half full of coffee and filled the other half with water to weaken it. I was one of the hands, so I had my coffee like everybody else. There was this huge platter of biscuits and another piled high with steaks. Also, there were three skillets of gravy on the stove. To me it looked like a meal fit for a king.

As we ate," Ole" Ross sat across from me along with the other cowhands, Billy, Leroy, Tom and some others whose names I don't recall. In the middle of the table was a kerosene lamp. It was only 4:30 in the morning and the sun wouldn't be up for about 20-30 minutes. By then we would be on our horses going about our day's work. There was no sitting up at night when you came in. You ate your supper and then went to bed.

Well, Ross took a look at the big pile of biscuits and then looked at me saying, "Now the newest and youngest feller in camp has to clean up all the biscuits and all the gravy. We can't have anything left."

Being a very obedient, dutiful young cowboy, I started eating. I would break up my biscuits, cover them with gravy and take another steak. They poured me another half cup of coffee and filled it on up with water. They were all just sitting watching me when Ross slapped his crippled leg with his crippled hand and began to laugh, which caused the rest to start laughing. I wanted to cry because I didn't know what they were laughing at. Finally, Ross said, "Now I am going to have to make a new batch of biscuits and gravy to feed the dogs. I didn't think you could eat that much!"

We had a bunch of old skinny poor cows that we'd gathered up out of the desert and we had trouble getting them to stay on their feet because they were more dead than alive. When we got to the top of the mountain, it was cooler and we left the cows, riding eight miles on down to camp where Ross had supper ready for us. We ate supper and then crawled into our chigoons (bed rolls) and went to sleep. We were above 10,000 feet and it was cold at night, but we were in a snug warm cabin.

When morning came, it was my job to go out and get what they called the night horse. We used the night horse to wrangle up the saddle and pack horses, which were in a pasture that was six miles across. The cowboys had put big cowbells on several of the horses. I would have to listen very carefully so when I heard the bells ring, I could make sure I was on the backside of them. If I wasn't, they would run to the far end of the pasture. If I was on the backside, they would run for camp.

At the camp, the cowboys were waiting. They would hear the cowbells ringing and would go out and open the gate. The horses would run into the big corral that covered an acre and a half. There was a smaller corral that was about 40 feet across that was the wrangling corral. This was where they would break any wild horses they caught. When I came down off the hill toward camp, there would always be a light in the door, which was always warm and inviting.

In any act of kindness there are those who are willing to go and be a part of it. When it came to the hard part of carrying Ross the 15 miles, there were enough people there; they could have taken turns and carried him a quarter of a mile at a time and nobody's arms would have gotten tired. They would have gotten there faster. It always remains, there's just a few that will carry the load, carry the hard part. My father was great in "Ole" Ross' eyes until his dying day as was Ralph and Doc. I was special to him as well because I was "Murray's boy."

Those three men were not church goers, but they had many Christian principles. They were honest, decent people. They fed the hungry and clothed the poor. When it came time to help somebody that was in trouble they were the first ones to offer a hand. They gave them beds to sleep in. They were the people that dug the graves, never charging a penny. They sat with the sick and dying just like my mother did. Jesus carried all of our burdens to the cross. He is there to carry us through all of our hard times.

DRY FORK FIRE

"That ole doe fought that fire 'til she droped dead, and her fawns died."

One summer when I was a kid, it was very dry. In the mountains when it's dry, lightning often starts forest fires. This particular summer a fire started in one of the canyons. In the beginning the fire burned slowly. It wasn't burning much, but then it began to move down the side of the mountain to where it was beginning to endanger ranches. The men decided it was time to start fighting the fire. They fought it for nearly a week before it was out.

As the men were fighting the fire, they noticed an old deer kept watching the fire. She would run up to the fire and stomp on it. She would run back and forth, paying no attention to the men at all. The men realized that she must have a fawn in the fire. When the fire was out, the men were walking by some burned trees and found two dead baby fawns. Later the mother would also die from the burns she suffered while trying to save her babies. I felt so sorry for the mother deer because she was trying to save her babies.

Jesus came to this world, fought sin and lost his life, but in losing his life, he rose again. Instead of us being charred hunks of humanity, if we give our lives to Jesus, he will save us in the Eternal Kingdom where there will be no death, sorrow or sadness. Please give your heart and life to Jesus. If you do, you will never have to worry about losing your life when surrounded by the fires of evil.

MATTIE AND SHAKE

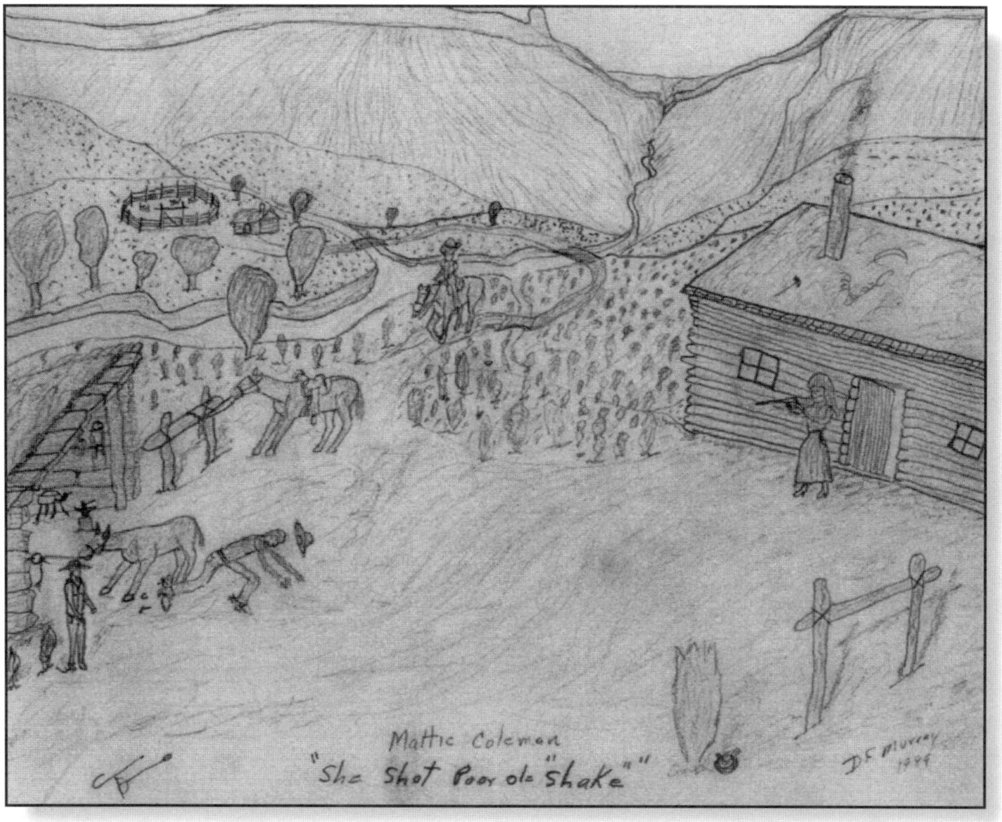

"She shot poor 'Shake'."

The little old lady dressed in black used to strike terror in the hearts of us young boys. After all, she was a gun slinging drunkard who had murdered her husband.

Shake and Mattie were an odd pair. Shake was long, lanky and thin. He was about 7 feet tall with long arms and long legs and weighed about 160 pounds. There was not a horse in the West that

Shake couldn't ride. Shake had a unique way, he could reach under their bellies with those long legs, hook his spurs together and there was no way a horse could throw him. He was a very homely individual.

In contrast, Mattie was a very petite, pretty little woman about 5 feet tall. Shake was a very easy going mellow person. Mattie was the opposite, she was a very high strung and quick tempered. Also, she had one bad habit, the habit of alcohol. When she got to drinking, she loved to play cards. She always won because people were afraid of her. She always had a gun handy, either a rifle or a Colt 45 six-shooter and she could use them both.

Mattie would go to town to a little pool hall where cards were played and you could buy a little alcohol to drink. There were a few pool tables, and as a young child I watched my father play cards in the same old pool hall where Mattie played cards.

Shake, to the contrary, would stand at the bar and drink a "sodie" pop or something like that, he was not an alcohol drinker. Mattie would play cards and get drunk and the drunker she got, the meaner she was. Finally, nobody would play cards with her and then she turned her anger on Shake. She would yell, "Shake, I'm going to kill you, you old so and so." He would throw his hands straight up in the air and say, "Blaze away little lady, blaze away." Well, she'd blaze away with the rifle, but she was always steady enough that she missed him even though sometimes she would leave a hole in his hat. If she had her handgun, she would begin to shoot at his feet and tell him to dance. "Dance, Shake dance" and he sure obliged. When Mattie was sober, she was a very sweet person, and loved Shake dearly. Shake was very much in love with Mattie, and when she got drunk he would say, "Oh go easy on the little lady boys, she means no harm."

Shake was an expert horseman. Not only could he ride horses, but he could also shoe horses. One day, Old Man Conwell and another neighbor rode up and asked Shake to shoe their horses. Shake was right in the middle of shoeing the horses when Mattie, who had been in the house drinking, came to the door with the rifle in her hands. She yelled, “Shake, I’m going to kill you.” Shake threw his arms up in the usual manner, reared back, laughed and said; “Blaze away little lady, blaze away.” Little by little her mind and reflexes had been affected by too much booze causing her to not be able to keep a steady hand as once she could. She cut down on him shooting him in the shoulder. He fell to the ground. Thinking she had killed him, she threw the gun down and ran screaming out in to the sagebrush. The neighbor looked after Shake while Old Con went to get Mattie. The neighbor took his red neckerchief, which he stuffed in the bullet hole to stop the bleeding. Old Con had to take his lariat, rope Mattie and drag her back like a calf to the branding fire.

After hog-tying Mattie, Old Con rode 5 miles to the neighbor, to get a pickup to haul Shake the 60 miles to the Doc. The model A Ford would travel about 30 miles per hour on the dirt Highway which today is a four lane interstate. They laid Shake on hay in the truck and they threw Mattie in beside him while Old Con sat on her like a sack of oats. All the way to town, Mattie kept swearing that she was going to kill Con.

When they arrived at the doctor’s office, they carried him in and laid him on the table. The doctor examined him and decided that he needed to operate immediately to take the bullet out of Shake’s shoulder. As the doctor reached for the ether, Shake grabbed Old Con’s pistol, which he stuck under the doctor’s nose. “You ain’t puttin’ me under until I deal with the sheriff about the Little Lady cause she never meant to hit me.” It took them about two hours to find the sheriff. When the sheriff arrived, Shake convinced him that it was an accident. By then, it had been over six hours and the loss of blood caused him to die on the operating table.

Mattie spent some time in the penitentiary. After she got out, her life completely changed. She gave up drinking, but, oh too late!

LAST OF THE FOOD

"Father always said to feed em." "Red gave that old Indian the last food he had in camp."

In Rio Blanco county in northern Colorado, is the little town of Meeker. Meeker was named after the man who had come there to set up an Indian agency to reform the Indians and make Christians out of them. This resulted in the great Meeker massacre and the annihilation of Thornberg and his troops. Josie Meeker, her mother and the other ladies were saved.

After the great massacre, the government moved the Ute Indians down to the White Rocks in Utah, but they would still come to the high mountains to hunt from time to time.

Red's family came to Rio Blanco County when Red was a tiny boy. Red's father had always been a frontiersman. He said, "feed the Indian and they will be happy."

Red talked about seeing seven or eight Indians with their ponies out in the yard sitting by a butchering vat, a big cast iron kettle, that you built a fire under to cook meat. Red's father always kept hot venison and beans cooked in it for when the Indians would come by. It didn't matter to them if the vat was covered with flies or not, they gladly ate the food.

One fall, Red's father and mother and the rest of the children went to town, which was 124 miles from their place. Red was just a small boy of six or seven and he was left at home to milk the cow and look after things. When they left, he had a big hunk of cheese and three or four loaves of homemade bread, which would be enough food to last him until they got back.

After the family arrived in town, a big blizzard hit which trapped them in town until the storm was over. Because of the delay, Red was nearly out of food. He had one little piece of cheese and two pieces of bread left when an old Indian rode in on an old broken down pony. He rubbed his stomach in the usual manner of wanting something to eat. Red took him into the little cabin, brought the cheese out of the cabinet along with the two slices of bread. He made a sandwich and handed it to him. The old Indian took the bread, opened it up, handed the cheese back, rubbed his stomach, pointed at Red and told him, "You eat."

Evening came and instead of getting on his old pony in the usual manner, the old Indian just stayed squatted down in the cabin, which had only one room. He leaned against the wall with his old Indian blanket wrapped around him. Next morning when Red got out of bed, there the old Indian sat. The old Indian got up and stretched, rubbed his stomach and said, "Me fine."

Red went to the barn to do his chores. When he returned to the house, the old Indian was no where in sight. Well, it wasn't long until the old Indian was back with a rabbit and he helped Red clean and roast it. They then sat down and ate. This continued for two weeks. Every morning while Red was doing his chores the old Indian would get up and go hunting. He would come back with a rabbit, grouse or a couple of trout.

One morning the old Indian was already gone when Red got up. Red went about his work but couldn't figure out where his Indian friend had gone. Red was sure getting lonely and feeling mighty small in the big wide open country. He had almost given up on his parents coming back and now his Indian friend was gone. He had finished evening chores and was trying to figure out what he would do for something to eat, when he heard the cracking of a whip and his father shouting at the team. After the return of Red's family, no one ever saw the old Indian again.

Red's father always got along with the Indians because he respected them as people. This kindness was repaid when the old Indian took care of Red. This kindness that Red learned from his father and the old Indian stayed with him through out the rest of his life. He never knew a stranger. He was always kind. He was a hard worker, but because of his generosity he didn't have much money. I met Red when we were working at the same place. He was doing odd jobs, whatever an old man could do.

The old time Westerners were not braggers. A few of them were liars, but most of them didn't care for lying or for bragging. They just kind of rambled on about the past. If you asked a question, they would shut up and say, "Well, it don't matter anyway." You wouldn't get any more out of them. As a child, I learned real early to sit and listen to the old time cowboys that came by our ranch while driving cattle to town.

The town in which I grew up was at one time the third largest shipping point in the country for livestock. My father's fields in the fall were always full of cows and the corrals were full of horses. The yard was full of bed rolls, and the house was full of cowboys. My mama always said, "When you have a cow hand in the house, you are in the hands of God." They weren't drunkards and revelers. They would come to town once in a while to celebrate a little, but they weren't anything like they portray them today. They were meek, quiet, very intelligent, thinking men. Many of them couldn't read or write and there where some who had high degrees, but there was one thing they all had in common, they respected God because they could see him in nature. They talked about the stars; they would talk about the trees, the rocks and the seasons and they would always wind up saying; "Look at this old pony I ride, nobody but a creator in heaven could make a pony like that."

This was Red's philosophy. One night Red got to telling me about the mine he used to work at when he was a young man. They were building the shoring and cribbing in this mine to keep it from caving in. They took huge timbers and set them upright and then made braces across and filled in behind.

They were in a very unstable area. They were working down in a deep tunnel when they heard a rumbling noise. Someone yelled, "Cave in!" The noise began to become deafening and all of a sudden, the dust began to choke them and they started to run. Well, they hadn't run far, when they came to this spot in the tunnel that was blocked off. As they got up on the rocks and began to dig, somebody could feel a draft of air coming through and said, "We can probably get through." They carefully dug their way through until they made a hole in the rubble. Red was the next to the last man to go through. As the last man started through, it caved in again, on top of the man's leg just below the knee. There he was stuck fast in the timbers and rocks. The rest of the men started moving rocks but every time they moved a rock, it seemed more began to fall and tighten up more on his leg. There seemed to be no way to get him loose. The seven or eight men that were with them said; "We're going to run; we're going to go before we all get trapped." They all took off leaving Red alone with the man pinned in the tunnel.

Red figured that his time was not up yet so he thought a little bit and took off his belt, which held his sharp axe. He tied this belt very tight around the man's leg and he said, "The only way we're going to get you out is to chop the leg off." The man agreed. Like all the old-timers and my father, Red kept his axe as sharp as a razor. He would sit and sharpen his knife and axe until you could peel the hair off your arm. With one mighty swing Red cut the leg off right above the knee. He picked him up, threw him over his shoulder and started running down the tunnel. Rocks were falling, but at last he reached the outside. When they emerged, the crowd roared in appreciation of Red's heroic deed to save the man. Those men who ran off and left them felt really ashamed. The man Red carried to safety was very thankful even though he had lost his leg.

We never know how our actions will affect others. Red's father treated the Indians with kindness, which the old Indian repaid when he took care of Red. The lessons Red learned from his father and the old Indian became the pattern for his life. Red developed his character and accepted the responsibility of doing the right things instead of what was easy and made him feel good. Therefore when Red saw the man trapped in the tunnel, he knew what he should do unlike the other men that were with him.

THE HORSE NOBODY COULD CATCH

Runnin the ole stud. "That ole pony could shore run. That trail was not a bridal path."

Charlie stood leaning against the corral looking through the rails at several cowboys, probably half a dozen or so, who were trying to catch one little brown horse. The little brown mare grew up in the wild until she got caught by some cowboys, along with the rest of her band of wild horses. She was a free spirited horse and didn't like the confinement of captivity. In the process of catching her, the cowboys had roped her and handled her roughly. Therefore the little mare had learned how to dodge a loop and to fight back until the cowboys considered her an outlaw, a very dangerous horse.

When the mare would run, the cowboys would throw their loop and just before the loop would go over her head, she would duck her head between her front legs and stop, spin around and go right back the same way she'd come. If they cornered her she would work on the fence until she'd put a hole in it and away she would go. This happened three or four times. Each time she took several other horses along. The cowboys fixed the fence and then ran all the horses back in. This went on for the better part of the day and the boss was so angry the last time she broke down the fence, he said, "I will give her to anybody who can catch her, and if nobody can, I'm going to kill her." After they had gotten the fence fixed and the horses were back in, everyone went to dinner except for Charlie.

This wise old rancher decided it was time to show these young boys a thing or to about catching this mare. He also was an exceptionally kind man who felt sorry for the mare.

In the bigger corral there was a tree about three feet away from the fence. He noticed several gentle old cow horses in the corral. He managed to move the mare from a smaller corral into the bigger corral in the following manner. He went to his truck and got a long rope. He cut the rope in half. Using one half, he hung it from the tree to the opposite fence leaving just a three foot opening between the tree and the fence. He then made a loop to catch her as she ran through the opening. He caught the two gentle mares and put them in the bigger corral behind the rope. He stepped into the big corral, leaving the gate open. When she saw the open gate, the little brown mare made a run for freedom, but ended up in the big corral with the other horses. Now Charlie took the lariat loop he had made earlier and hung it on the fence and to the tree so it would come off. On the opposite end, he ran it down the fence tying it to a post by the gate, which would still give the little mare about 20 foot of slack. Well, he stepped down in the corral and she was willing to fight. She ran up and saw the rope hanging in the large area between the tree and fence. Then she saw the opening between the tree and the fence where the lariat was hanging. She went through there just as hard as she could run with the loop settling around her neck. She made about thirty feet, and came to the end of the rope, which tightened up and threw her, flopping her on the ground. Charlie ran over and sat on her head before she had time to get up. If you sit on a horse's head and hold it down, they can't get up. He covered her eyes, talking and petting her. She was sweating and trembling, but she wouldn't fight.

He waited until the men came out from dinner. He hollered, "I need some help." So they got him a good strong halter. He fastened the other rope that was tied to the tree and the fence through the halter and up around her neck so that it wouldn't choke her. After doing the same with the other rope, he got off her head and let her up. Well, she began to fight, jump, lunge and try to get away, but every time she did, there was a man on each end of the rope tightening the rope, until finally they had her at the gate.

They backed a trailer up to the gate, tied her tight with one rope and put the other rope through the trailer. They put the rope coming through the trailer on a good strong horse and pulled her right in. Charlie then hooked his truck to the trailer and pulled the mare home to the middle of his pasture. There he unhooked his truck from the trailer and left it sitting there with the little mare in it. He carried her feed and water morning and night, talking to her and trying to get her to eat grain. Finally, after two or three days she began to eat oats, which horses love to eat. After a while, her fear left her and she would no longer try to get away when she saw Charlie coming.

One morning, he reached in and pulled her over tight to the side of the trailer and took off one of the ropes. He tied that rope to the end of the other one and ran it out through the back door. Then he tied it to a wagon with about three hundred feet of rope so she had plenty of room to graze. He opened the trailer gate and she took off as hard as she could run. When she hit the end of the rope, she flipped and landed on her side.

Every morning he would go out and water her. She began to like grain. He would make her come up to him to get the grain. He would stand back just a few feet out of the way while she ate her grain. To keep grass for her, he would hook on to the wagon every morning with a jeep and move it. In doing so, she would brace her feet. She wasn't going to move, but he kept going any way. The jeep was stronger than her so she had to go along. In this way, Charlie broke her to lead.

Three or four months went by, and when Charlie came carrying her water, she'd be glad to see him. By then, spring came. He decided that she needed to be free, but he still wasn't ready to take off the rope. He now tied it to a heavy log. When she ran to the end, it would give and she wouldn't hit the ground so hard. She learned how to duck her head and drag that log all over the pasture. Finally, Charlie could take hold of the rope and lead her.

By the time fall came, he'd had her a whole year. She would lead and wouldn't fight him. Charlie put her in the corral by the barn where he was able to sweet talk her into the barn with the help of some oats. He would tie her there and then he would stand on the opposite side of a panel. Then he would feed her grain.

Breaking wild horses. "He shore was a prayin."

The first time he touched her he used a glove on a stick. He laid it on her back and she just had a fit. She tried to bite it as well as kick. After a while, she began to let him brush and curry her. One day he laid an old rug on her back. She didn't like that much, but she didn't fuss very long because she was eating her grain. It got so he could do anything around her as long as she was eating her grain.

One day Charlie laid a saddle on her back. The mare didn't fuss because she got used to having Charlie lay stuff on her back. However when he tightened up the cinch and turned her into the corral, she'd had enough of that contraption. She bucked as hard as she could, squealing the whole time until she became so tired that she could no longer buck. Then she lay down and rolled trying to get rid of the saddle. When this didn't work, she got up, walked over to the fence and started rubbing the saddle on the fence. This worked better. The saddle caught on a post and she was free of that contraption.

A few days later she had a colt. She was a good mother as most range horses are. The first thing Charlie did when he saw the colt was to put a halter on it. Then he taught the colt to lead. When he would lead the colt, the mare ran after him, crying for her baby. This gave Charlie an idea. Every time he saddled the mare, she went to bucking. He thought if he took the colt out of the corral and started to lead it away, the mare would worry more about what was happening to her colt and forget the saddle. When Charlie put his plan in effect it worked like a charm. He saddled the mare and turned her loose. The mare went to bucking as usual. While she was doing this, Charlie led the colt out of the corral into the pasture. When the mare realized that the colt wasn't following her in all her bucking antics, she came running after them. It wasn't too long until she forgot all about this bucking business.

By the time Charlie had her three years, he was putting a pack saddle on her. He told me he was going to use her as a pack horse. Well, this worked out fine. I'm sure he eventually rode her.

We think that we have to have the freedom to do as we please. We fight any restraint that Christ puts on us as the mare fought Charlie. We need to realize that these restraints are for our own good. When we submit to the kindness of Christ and feed upon his word as this little mare did her grain, all the things that cause us trouble will disappear. Soon we become dependable Christians that can be trusted in any circumstances to stand up for the word of God. Then, we can treat others with the same kindness that Charlie used on the little mare.

HORNET'S NEST

"Ole Hatch shore put Sam in a bind." "He hit the nest with his quirt and then loped on."

If we study nature we can find out many things that scientists spend millions of dollars to learn. Sometimes they come up with the same conclusions the cowboys did. Many cowboys couldn't even write their name, but they understood a lot about nature. They could tell how much snow they would get in the winter by observing the yellow jacket hornet's nest. If it was going to be real cold with not much snow, the hornet's nest would be low in the brush, close to the ground. If they were going to have a lot of snow, the nest would be way up high in the brush. It was only by God's grace that the hornet could know where to put the nest.

My grandfather was not a very kind or gentle man. He had a very cruel sense of humor. One day Grandfather and young Sam were out riding. Sam had 4 pack horses tied behind his horse. Grandfather was in the lead and he knew Sam's pack horses were slow. If they didn't want to run, they didn't. When Grandfather went by this hornet's nest, he took his riding whip and popped the nest, then spurred his horse and away he went.

Sam came along a bit later and there was the nest right beside the trail. By then, those hornets were very, very angry. All of a sudden there were hornets all over Sam, all over his horse, and the pack horses were each trying to go a different way.

When Sam finally got down to where Grandfather was, Grandfather was laughing as if it was the funniest thing in the world. Sam's eyes swelled shut and he was lucky he didn't die from all those hornet stings.

Sometimes Satan tempts us to think that doing something cruel is fun. It might seem funny, but we ought to stop and think very carefully what the consequences of our actions are. We are responsible for every thing we do. Ask your self what would Jesus do in this situation?

SAVING THE TAXPAYER MONEY

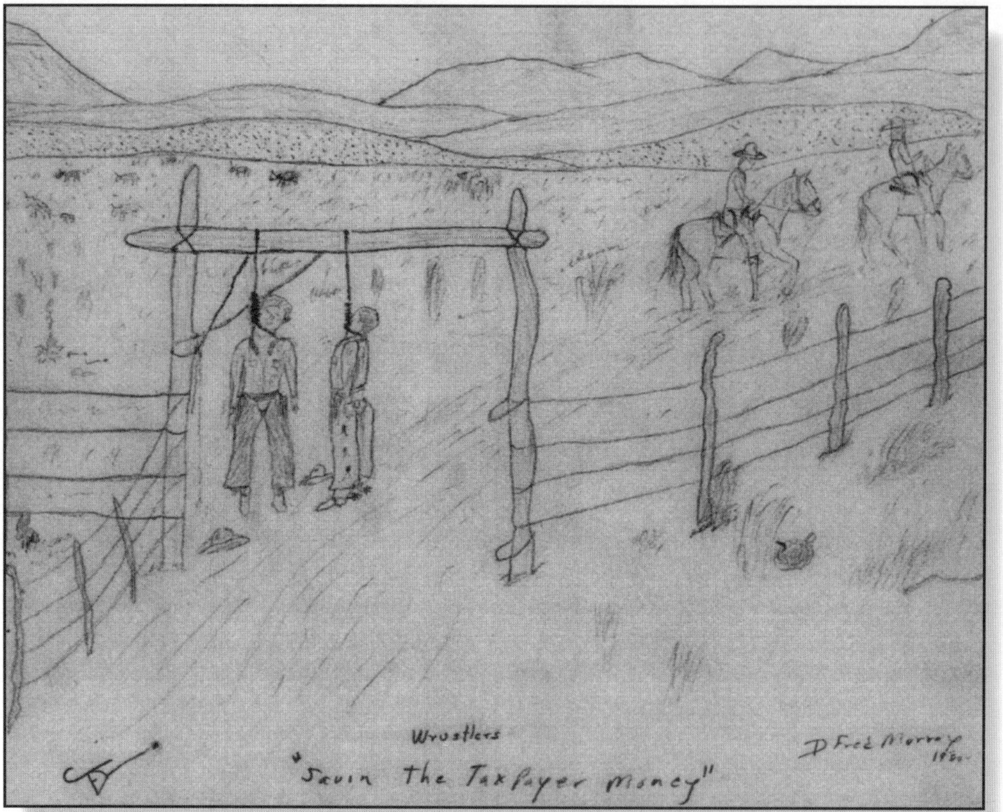

Wrustlers. "Savin the taxpayer money."

In the northwest corner of Colorado, the southwest corner of Wyoming, and the northeast corner of Utah lies a valley known as Brown's Hole. It is just below the famous Flaming Gorge Dam that is on the Green river. The valley cuts across the three states of Colorado, Wyoming and Utah, so it was a stronghold for outlaws for many years.

Before then, Jim Bridger from Fort Bridger would bring cattle to the valley and winter them there. It was beautiful high mountain country. It was close enough to the desert that the winters were mild most of the time. The cattle could winter out.

It wasn't long until the frontier people like the Bassett's and Billy Wert and others came into the country to settle it. Queen Ann Bassett and Josie Bassett were the first white children born in that country. They were rugged individualists that people called "Queen of the Outlaws" and other things, but they were just people living their lives not realizing they were making history.

Into this country, there came outlaws such as Butch Cassidy, Tom Horn and Matt Warner. Butch Cassidy and his bunch were not killers. They terrorized people, but they never took lives. Now Tom Horn was a paid killer. He was a bounty hunter who loved to kill. Bob Meldron was another one that came to Snake River Wyoming and to Brown's Hole to hire his gun out. They never faced a man as the movies show them today. Oh no, they hid in the bushes and cowardly shot people in the back.

My grandfather used to tell me the story of thirteen year old Willie Strange. Willie's father was a mining engineer, but his health failed him while working in the mines in Kentucky so he moved his family west, settling in Brown's Park. He prospected for different types of ore and barely made enough for his family to survive. Willie's mother died of pneumonia.

When spring came, Willie's family was out of supplies. It was sixty miles to the nearest town that you could get to in early March, and that was Rock Springs, Wyoming. Father left Willie at home because they didn't need the extra weight, but the older brother went along to help. It would take three days to get to Rock Spring, Wyoming because the roads were still muddy and still had snow in them, but it was necessary to get supplies.

Down on the river was an old man who was a former slave who ran the ferry. He was kind of a speckled man, and people called him Albert Speck. Speck wasn't his last name, but that is what they called him so that is what he went by. He always had the theory, "I'se too busy minding my own business to get into any anybody's else's." He saw good men come by and he saw bad men, but he always minded his own business. So Father Strange left Willie there and told him; "Now Willie, you stay here with Albert and don't go off with any cowboys."

The supply trip would take Willie's father about two weeks. For two or three days Willie hung around the ferry and there wasn't that many people crossing. He listened to all the stories Albert told about his life as a young slave boy; following General Sherman, running after him to thank him for setting them free and how he traveled to the West. Willie tired of the old stories because he had heard them so many times before when his father was down at Albert's store.

There were three bad men named Johnson, Lant and Tracy as well as their friend Bennett. Bennett hung around the others, but he really wasn't that bad a man, but the other three had been in the Utah prison until they overpowered a guard, escaped and came to Brown's Park.

One day Tracy, Lant and Johnson rode in. They thought it was fun to put Willie up on their horses. They fascinated Willie and they made him feel important as if he was a man. They laughed, joked and had a lot of fun with this thirteen year old boy. When evening came, they just went and got a horse for him to ride. Now, knowing them, they probably stole it somewhere, but they gave Willie his own horse. He was going to be a cowboy just like them.

Well, everything was fine for a day or two until these three cowboys got roaringly drunk one night. When Willie woke up in the morning, he couldn't get them awake. He went to get the water bucket. It was a cold March day and the bucket of water had ice on it. He just took a big dipper of the ice water and threw it right in Lant's face, the worst person to throw it on, the meanest of killers. He jumped up and was going to shoot the boy. The other two said, "Let's not get into killing a kid. We can get somebody better than that." So they talked it over and they decided they would make him do a dance. So they

Brown's Park hangin. "They went in and ate supper." "That was the Utah Posse."

took him outside and told him to run to Albert Specks. Willie took off and they shot at his heels. They were doing pretty well, but because their minds were numbed by the alcohol, one of them hit him in the back. It went in the spine and on up through a lung. The people from the ranch where they were staying came out and did all they could for Willie, but a few hours later Willie died.

There was a good family by the name of Hoy that lived in the community and Valentine, one of the young men who had gone to college in Paris, was appointed as magistrate, the local law and judge of Brown's Hole. They came and got him and when they got back to the ranch, these three scoundrels were gone.

They dispatched somebody to Hahn's Peak, which is just north of Steamboat Springs, a good sixty or seventy miles away. The sheriff left Steamboat Springs in a sled. When they got about forty miles West, they came to the little town of Lay. They could go no farther because the snow was melting, so they borrowed a spring wagon.

The next afternoon as they neared Brown's Park, the sheriff saw three men ride off the road and up in the hills. He thought about checking them out, but without a saddle horse he couldn't have caught them. He proceeded another fifteen miles down to the ranch, where he got the whole story and realized who he was dealing with. Early the next morning there was a posse of about twenty or thirty men including the Wyoming sheriff. My grandfather was Sheriff Pope's deputy out of Uintah county Utah, so he sent my grandfather and two other deputies to help. They went over Diamond Mountain instead of going around because it would save half a days ride.

Now Diamond Mountain was an interesting place. It got its name because someone said they found diamonds on the mountain. Some men bought up the land and then spread the word that the mountain contained diamonds all over it. Many men rushed to the area and wanted to buy the land, which they graciously sold for a great price. A few found the diamonds that the crooks planted, but no one made a fortune except for the bunch that sold the land. Of course, the men who sold the land disappeared before anyone discovered the scam. It was one of the great hoaxes of the West. Despite the phony claims, the name Diamond stuck. It served as a good reminder that nothing in this life is free. Anything of value takes a lot of hard work to achieve. If someone tries to tell you other wise, you better watch out because they are likely trying to con you.

After crossing the mountain and reaching the valley, they ran into Bennett who led three pack horses. Thinking that Bennett was one of the gang, they disarmed him, put a rope around his neck while he sat on his horse and tied the rope to the nearest gate post. Then they led his horse away. Later they learned that Bennett was not there when Willie was murdered. Some said Bennett was leaving the country because he was afraid that his past dealings with the murderers would cause him to be blamed as well, which is what happened. However, My grandfather always believed that Bennett was taking supplies to the murderers, which made him an accomplice. Therefore Grandfather felt he had done the right thing by hanging the man. He said, "We just saved the taxpayer some money."

After hanging Bennett, they proceeded on to the Bassett Ranch where they set up the headquarters for the posse. People fanned out through the hills in all directions looking for the murderers. Finally, they came across these three outlaws holed up on a cliff. From their vantage point, they could see when anyone was approaching and would cut down on the posse when it tried to get close. Valentine Hoy, being a good, peaceful man decided to reason with these bad men. He took off his gun and walked unarmed in to the open. He told them; "I just want to talk to you; I'm unarmed." He kept his hands and arms out so they could see them. When he got within about 20 feet, they shot him down in cold blood. The three men had the advantage as they were above everybody and could see the whole country. If anybody got too close they could kill them. There was just no way to get them. They'd left their horses at the bottom of the mountain. As the lawmen slipped through the brush and around rocks to avoid getting hit, they found the three horses. They took the horses with them and left the three men a foot in the cold March weather. Maybe they'd have a chance to either freeze them or starve them out. These hardened men did not intend to be frozen, starved or caught. They proceeded down off the mountain after dark and down to the river. The next morning when the posse went out to look for them, they could see their tracks. The killers got to the river, which was covered with ice. They walked about 20 miles on the ice. When they got to Ledore canyon the water was so rough and fast that no ice covered the water so they had to turn around and go back.

About the time they got off the ice and up the mountain, they saw an old wild mare with a baby colt. Two of the men's boots wore out so they shot this colt and had a meal of the raw meat and made themselves some shoes out of the green hide. In the cold weather their hide shoes soon froze. They went on until finally they couldn't walk any farther and by then the sheriff's posse from the three states caught up with them. After a shoot-out they finally surrendered. The three men were hungry, wet, cold and their feet hurt. The two wearing the hide shoes couldn't get them off their frozen feet.

On the way back, Lant, who had his regular boots on, got his hands free without being seen, reached down and slid the bridle off his horse, which was being lead by a deputy. Lant kicked the horse and it took off as hard as it could run. He surprised the posse so much that they had no time to shoot him and he got away.

After they took the other two in, they spent the rest of the day looking for Lant, but they couldn't find him. When they found him the next day they were unable to capture him because he had enough ammunition to hold them off.

The deputy of the Colorado posse had custody of one of the men and the Wyoming posse was holding the other man at another ranch. The Utah posse cut the sleeves off their slickers and pulled them over their heads as masks. They disarmed the Colorado deputy and tied him to the chair. Then they took the murderer out and hanged him.

They finally caught Lant and took him and the other man to Colorado. The Colorado sheriff said, "You can't have them because we caught them, they were in Colorado." The Colorado sheriff didn't want to lose them so he took them to the town of Hahn's Peak and they riveted a steel cell and put them in it.

In four or five days, they tricked the guard who brought "em feed." They beat the guard almost to death and then they escaped.

The next three months is a long, sordid story of what happened to the two men. One was finally killed, but Lant made it to Walla Walla, Washington. There the lawmen surrounded him in a wheat field. He kept shooting at them and they couldn't get close so they just made a big circle around him out of range of his rifle. Then they set the wheat field on fire and that ended that.

Because of one boy's disobedience, twenty-four people (20 of them innocent) lost their lives in one of the worst killing sprees of the West.

BARBED WIRE TREACHERY

"Waiting for Mama." "The curse of the western range."

In the eyes of an old time cowboy, barbed wire was the worst curse that ever was. At the time it came into use, they didn't realize it would be necessary in civilizing the West by keeping the farmers' fields separate to raise grain and produce, but along with everything that's good there is generally something bad. There is an old saying in the West, "it's not all good and it's not all bad," and it makes sense if you think about it.

The wild and range horses ran free on pastures that were 25-30 thousand acres. It was nothing to have a pasture that was 30 miles across with no fences. The treachery of barbed wire was that the farmers and ranchers used it to build drift or pasture fences that blocked the old animal trails. Since the horses ran freely down the trails, many of them would get tangled up in the wire as they weren't expecting to suddenly come upon something in their path.

Not only have I seen horses injured and killed by the barbed wire, I've seen many deer killed in their attempt to jump the fence. The deer's hind legs went between the wires and the legs would become so tightly twisted that the deer would hang. If you found a deer hanging you could sometimes cut them loose, but they would generally charge you. The best way to get them loose was to ride your horse to the opposite side of the fence, reach down, cut the wire and take off as hard as your horse could run. However, most often by the time we found them, they were dead.

One of the saddest memories I have is of finding an old range mare tangled in the barbed wire fence. The mare bled to death leaving her little colt waiting for its mother. The colt was more dead than alive and in the bushes you could see the coyotes waiting for it to become weaker or die while overhead the buzzards were flying. I know this is nature's way but it is a picture that is imprinted upon my mind of the cruelties of life.

We must watch barbed wire fences in life. We too can become entangled in these barbed wire fences in life and lose our lives. We must watch for them. It can be recklessly driving a car, rushing across a street without looking, or trying drugs or alcohol. If we ask Jesus every day to give us strength to watch for these barbed wire fences of life, we can be prepared for them and by not running blindly, stop in time.

HUNG UP

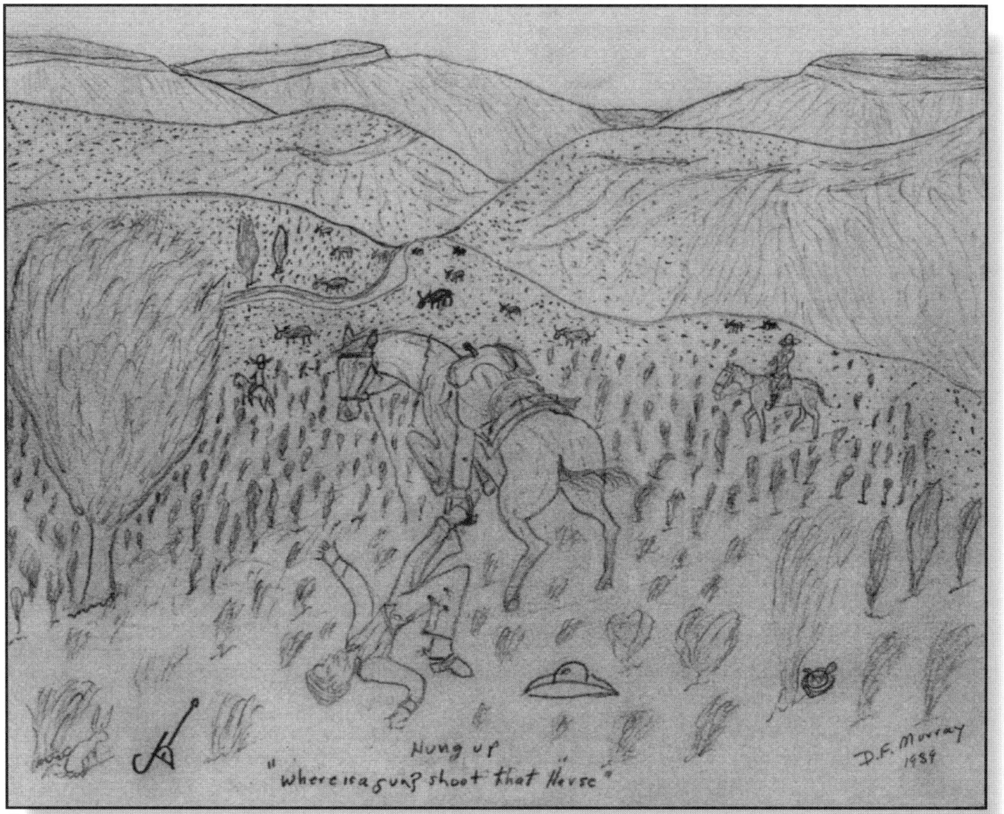

"Where is a gun? Shoot that Horse."

Have you ever wondered why cowboys wear high heeled boots? It isn't for looks, but for protection. The heel keeps the foot from sliding through the stirrup. Occasionally, if a horse bucked real hard, a person could get caught on the saddle.

I worked for a ranch owner named Russ who told me this story. Russ had a dandy gray mustang he had caught out on the open range.

The colt broke "out" real good except for one bad habit. When one least expected it, he might go to bucking. The true cowboy felt if a horse didn't buck a little bit, it wasn't any good. It needed to have a little buck in it occasionally, so the cowboys would hoot, holler, wave their hats and spur him on. Soon the horse got tired of it and quit. This was all part of the day's fun.

One day Russ was riding his gray horse when it went to bucking. While bucking, the horse started down a hill, which caused the horse to stumble. The horse regained his footing, but Russ fell off. However one of his feet caught in the stirrup and one spur caught in the cinch. The horse was dragging him, kicking Russ in the back and in the head.

In this situation, most cowboys would have shot the horse because a man's life is worth more than an animal. However, the two young "fellers" that were with Russ were greenhorns and didn't know enough to take out their guns and shoot the horse. At last one of them finally cut the horse off, stopped it and unsaddled him.

Russ was more dead than alive. They went back to camp to get another gentle horse. They laid Russ across the back of the gentle horse and took him the 20 miles to the ranch. When they got there, they thought he was dead, but he was alive. Russ recovered but he had many back problems and pain in his neck and shoulder.

I was in Colorado a few years ago and saw Russ. Russ was an old man in his 90's. He was still straight and tall. He could laugh and talk about getting hung up in the saddle or running wild horses. We talked about the good times we used to have when I was a kid.

Sometimes in life, Satan would have us get hung up, maybe on money, on clothes, on appetite, on pride or worldly lust. We may have to take a kicking or abuse, not as the horse would give us, but to humble us and let us realize that God loves us and cares for us.

TRAGEDY OF WILD HORSE RUNNING

"There he sat leanin against the tree dead, the rope on both horses and around his neck."

There was a family that lived in the next valley, which was about 50 miles from us. In the West, we considered people living that close to be neighbors because there were so few people. They had two boys named Phil and Bobby who were a little older than me. The boys helped their folks on the ranch as well as working on other ranches. The thing they loved the most to do was to "run wild horses," which is how we described catching wild horses. They caught wild horses when they had time whether summer or winter. The horses caught would bring from 10-15 dollars.

The two brothers along with two other cowboys set out one cold winter morning to see if they could catch some horses. The snow was deep on the ground, which was the best time to catch mustangs because they were weak and hungry. The cowboys always rode grained, well-fed horses giving them plenty of strength and stamina. It was not long until they came across several bands of wild horses with each cowboy going in a separate direction.

Soon each cowboy roped a mustang and tied it to a tree where they would come back later to get it. They planned to meet at a certain place. All arrived safely except Bobby. It was getting late in the day so they decided to go back to the ranch because it was getting dark. When they returned to the ranch, they found that Bobby had not arrived home.

Very early the next morning, A large number of cowboys went looking for Bobby. Several miles from where they first saw the wild horses the day before, they found Bobby setting by a tree. He had his horse's bridle reins in his hands. When they got close enough, they could see that he had caught a wild horse that was on the end of his rope and dallied on Bobby's saddle. The rope was around the tree and his neck. Bobby was dead.

There are many tragedies in life that we do not understand. Bobby was doing his job when his horse stumbled and fell. We must not blame God for such tragedies. This is part of the world we live in. It is very sad when a young man's life is cut short as Bobby's was.

WINTER TRAVEL

"Four feet of snow, forty below zero, a sick wife and eight children, one hundred and forty miles took five days."

My mother whose name is Luella told me this story. When she was a young girl about 14 years old, her family lived in a valley in Western Colorado. Her mother became very ill, so Luella sat down and wrote to her grandmother, telling her of her mother's illness.

Her grandparents lived 130 miles away, which was a long distance when the only means of travel was by horse or if you were lucky and the roads were dry you could drive a Model T Ford. They did most of the traveling by horse and wagon in the summer and horse and sled in the winter.

Just before Thanksgiving, Luella's grandmother caught the horse drawn mail stage down to the valley. She came to take care of her daughter. She was there a while and could see her daughter was not improving so just after Christmas, she wrote her husband to come and bring a team and sled.

Luella's grandfather hooked up six horses to a wagon. He put a cover on it and put in a little stove to keep the wagon warm and to cook on. He got behind the hole in the curtain and drove down to the valley. It took him five days to go the 130 miles with the team and wagon. Because of the way the sun would shine on the snow in the morning, the mountain roads would be muddy by afternoon, if the clouds cleared as they generally did. The last 30 miles was on the sunny side of the mountain and the mud was terrible.

He stayed a couple of days so they could prepare the wagons. They put an extra tarp over the top to make it warmer and put in a supply of wood. They made a cot in there for Luella's mother to lie on.

Luella's grandparents, mother and the other eight children still at home were in one wagon. Her father brought the furniture in another wagon pulled by a six horse team.

The morning they left, it was 26 degrees below zero, but by the middle of the day it began to warm up. They had to plow mud for about 20 miles. It wasn't deep mud, but it pulled the horses hard. They made 30 miles the first day. They reached Rifle, Colorado at 8 o'clock. The thermometer on the bank read 26 below zero.

Luella's grandfather pulled up to the hotel and carried his daughter into her room. Then he and Luella's father went to the livery stable to take care of the horses.

The first day was easy compared to what lay ahead. The next morning they started over Government Pass. They went up to about 10,000 feet and the snow was about 5 feet deep. The horses would lunge and break through the snow to make a path. Then they stopped and rested.

When they stopped and rested, Luella's grandfather would dig down in the snow, getting sagebrush to build a fire. Everyone had on all the clothes they owned and they wrapped up in blankets. They were cold, but they survived.

They spent the second night on a side of a mountain by some pine trees in the snow. They cleaned the snow back and built a big fire and fixed their rations. All the horses had to eat was oats.

About 2 o'clock the next afternoon they arrived in Meeker, Colorado. The thermometer on the bank said it was 36 degrees below zero.

The fourth night, they spent out on Yellow Jacket Pass. The snow was between 6 and 8 feet deep. The only way they could get through some of the drifts was for one of the men to lead the horses while the other man followed with a whip. They made the horses lunge, plunge and break through the snow. Then they turned them around and drove them back through the path they had made. The snow would be broken so the other horses could get through.

The fifth evening, they were down in Axel Basin at the Buchanan Ranch. The Buchanan Ranch was one of the first small ranches in the basin. Members of the Buchanan family still operate the ranch.

The people of the West always took in people that didn't have any place to go. They put blankets on the floor and built a big fire in the stove. It was warm in their log cabins. They fed their horses hay and cared for the animals. They always prepared a good meal of potatoes, pancakes, eggs and bacon, which gave them plenty of energy. They warmed rocks to put in the wagons to keep the travelers' feet warm. The Buchanan's were good people.

They made it to Luella's grandparents place about midnight on the sixth night. There wasn't any place in the canyon to stay. Going up out of the canyon was a hard pull. They just kept going even though the horses were about worn out.

Luella's mother got better, but what a terrible trip that must have been. They must have been cold, but they never complained.

Back then, people never blamed the government or anyone else for their problems. They just did the best they could and they survived. You know they had faith. They were good Christian people. On this trip, they asked God for help, strength and wisdom. They asked God to give their teams strength. When they were having trouble getting through the snow drifts, they asked God to help them. If we ask, God will help us in any situation we find ourselves.

"For He shall give his angels charge over you, to keep you in all your ways." Psalms 91:11

FORK IN THE NOSE

"She shore gave that fork a yank." "I just stood there crying."

We were getting ready to go to my aunt's house for Christmas dinner, when my father told me to "throw the cows a little more hay." I climbed the ladder to the top of the big haystack. Being in a hurry to go, I was pitching the hay as fast as I could over the fence when the fork slipped out of my hand and went flying right toward an old cow that was below me eating hay. There was nothing I could do but watch as the fork shot toward that old cow's nose. When the four pronged spear hit the bullseye (or in this case the "cowseye"), that old cow started spinning like a top. I could not get near the cow, so I ran to the house crying. Mother met me at the door dressed in her best clothes, a fur coat, a beautiful hat and high-heeled shoes, and asked; "What's wrong?" I then blurted out what happened.

Mother was the only woman I ever saw who could run on three inch high heels. Not waiting for Father, she lit out after that old cow like a dog after a rabbit with me following. When mother got to the corral, the old cow stood with her head down with the pitchfork still sticking out of her nose. Mother ran up, stuck her heels in the ground, grabbed the fork with both hands and gave the fork a jerk, pulling it free from the cow's nose.

That old cow thanked Mom by lowering her head and knocking Mom right down in the snow! I waved my hands and chased the cow away. Mom got up and dusted the snow off her coat and we soon took off for my Aunt's house to eat Christmas dinner. Every time that cow saw my mother, she showed her appreciation by butting, kicking or knocking Mom down. Somehow that cow got it in her mind that mother was the one who had stabbed her with the pitchfork.

Don't be like that old Cow, make sure you don't blame the wrong person. If someone does a good deed for you, always be thankful.

SHOT AT SUPPER

"That Indian killed poor ole 'Ary'."

The Bible tells us that if we have something against someone, we should talk to them. If they don't want to talk to you, take someone else along to mediate. Then if they don't want to talk, just leave them alone.

As a young boy, my mother's brother Ira lived in Montana. He and an Indian boy went to school together. Ira and the Indian boy had an argument, but Ira just passed it off and forgot all about it.

After he grew up, Ira married and had three children. He had a big ranch where he raised fancy horses that he sold in the East for polo ponies. He was comfortably wealthy and doing well.

One night the family was all sitting at the table eating when the kitchen door opened and there stood that Indian with a rifle. He shot Ira point blank in the chest. The family called the sheriff, but by the time he got there Uncle Ira was dead.

When the sheriff got back to town the Indian was sitting in his office. He confessed to shooting Ira. The Indian said, "I am glad Ira's dead and I don't care if you hang me."

At the trial, he told that when he and Ira were small children going to grade school they got in an argument. The Indian held a grudge over this for over twenty years and decided to get even by shooting Ira. That particular day he had been drinking and in a drunken rage he took his gun and murdered Ira.

It never pays to hold a grudge. Sometimes it destroys others, but the person it usually destroys is yourself. When we feel we have been cheated or wronged, we should stop and think about Jesus. He healed and helped people, but the people yelled, "crucify him." They hanged him on the cross. Live your own life. Don't worry about what others do to you. In the long run, if you live a virtuous life, you will be rewarded.

CUTTING THE WATER HOLE

"Ole Jim shore fell thru the ice." The railroad bar fell across the hole, that's what saved him." They would have never found him, it was 20° below."

When I was a young man, we didn't have heated water tanks for our livestock. We didn't even have running water in the house. We carried water from the Colorado River.

Then, It was a big, clear, beautiful river. It was a good quarter of a mile across and it was 10-15 feet deep. Now, the Colorado River is just a small stream because the utility companies divert the water for drinking water in many cities. Also, farmers and ranchers use the water for irrigation.

In the winter, slush ice floated across the whole river except for about 8-15 feet along the edge. The ice would freeze up to a foot and a half thick. If we didn't cut a hole in the ice close to the edge, the cattle would walk out on the ice to get a drink. If they walked out on the ice, their weight would cause the ice to break, dumping them into the river where they would drown.

Therefore early every morning we chopped a hole in the ice as every night it would freeze solid again. We used an axe, shovel and big six foot long steel railroad bar to cut through the ice. You would chop the ice with your axe, then take the bar and turn the ice upside down on the edge or push it under. The water under the water hole might be 4-5 feet deep and it was very swift.

It was my little brother Jim's job to cut the hole in the ice since I no longer lived at home and my father was quite ill. One morning it was about 35 below zero when Jim went to cut the hole in the ice. He had on his heavy winter clothes, a big heavy sheepskin coat and two pairs of clothes, long underwear, heavy boots, a cap and mittens.

While he was digging the hunks of ice from the hole with the bar, he slipped and fell into the ice cold water. He had the bar in his hands when he slipped and the bar fell cross ways over the hole, which kept him from drowning. If he didn't quickly get out of the frigid water, he would likely freeze to death in just a few minutes. He hollered and hollered, but the house was a quarter of a mile away so no one heard his cries for help. He kept trying to pull himself out, but he would slip into the water. He didn't have the strength to get out and with each try he became weaker. The angels of God were looking out for him. Feeling desperate, with no help in sight, he started to pray. When he finished praying, he gave it one more try and with a burst of strength God gave him the strength to pull himself out of the icy water.

No matter what bad situation you get in, Jesus is there to pull you out if you will ask for his help.

HERDING MILK COWS

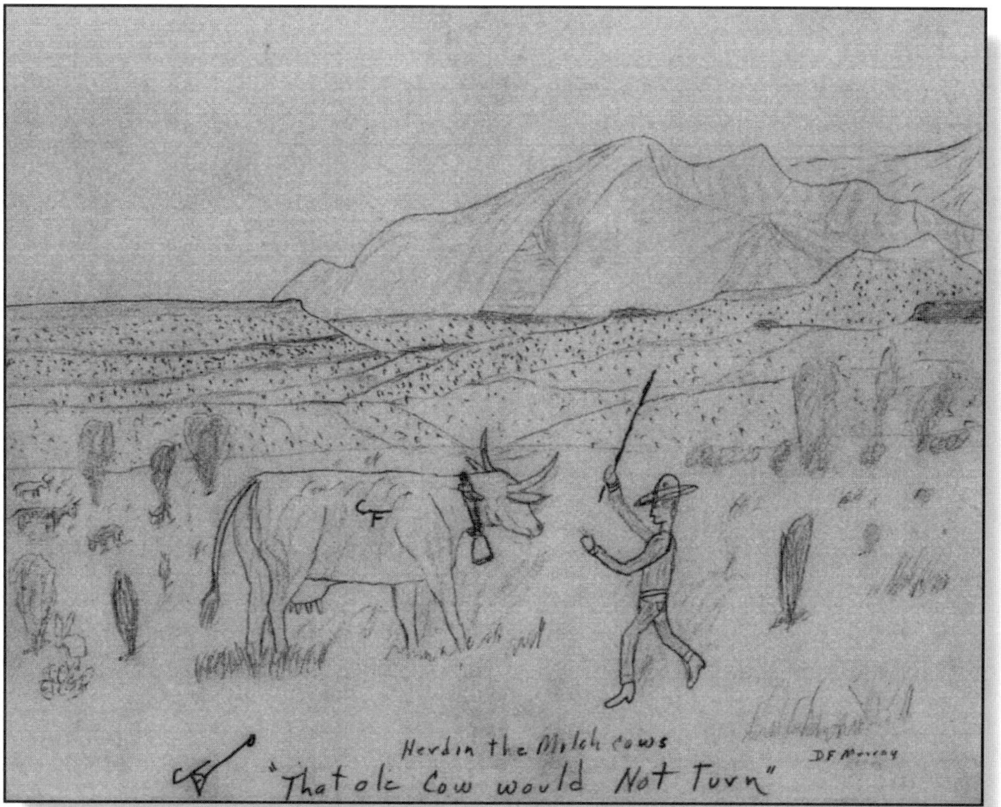

"That ole cow would not turn."

In our desert valley the irrigation water ran off the fields into the road ditches, which always made for plenty of grass. It was the job for the children of the community to take the milk cows and herd them along in the roads.

I was a little boy, I suppose I was four years old when I first started herding the milk cows. Mother would pack me a lunch and I would get a drink out of the irrigation ditch, this was in the days before we knew about pollution. We milked the cows every day, morning and evening. We had nice sweet cream to put on our cereal and nice warm milk to drink. Also, Mama made cottage cheese and American cheese.

We had three milk cows. On one old Jersey cow, Dad put a bell around her neck, which supposed to tell us where she was, but she could walk for miles without ever ringing the bell. She would hold her neck perfectly still and not make it clank. That old cow was always the leader. Sometimes I met the neighbor boys and all our cows would get mixed up. When it would come time to go home, this old Jersey bell cow of ours would get to her feet; clang the bell and take off running in the opposite direction from home; leading the rest of the cows with her. There was no way we could turn them around and get them back. She would get them in the high sagebrush; where they could hide from us and of course, there would be no sound of a bell.

It would come time to milk and no boys would be home with the cows. That's when we would get in trouble for playing around and not herding the cows. Our parents forbid us to let our cows mix. However, that old cow wouldn't go, she'd start running and I'd stand in front of her. I'd beat her with my stick, kick her on the nose and she just knocked me down as if I wasn't even there.

When she started off in the other direction, I finally learned to grab her by the bell strap that was around her neck. I kept the bell ringing and mother would hear and come to help. As soon as the old cow saw my mother she would turn and just walk home as good as could be. The bell would ring all the way home. She knew when there was somebody big that she had to obey, but she knew she could run over me.

You know the devil knows he can run over us, but if we clang the bell loud enough by praying to Jesus, he will come running to help as my mother did to help me when she heard the ringing bell.

THRESHING TIME

Catching the Runaway. "Ole Charlie could run as fast as a horse." He was the only man that could run down a runaway."

When I see the great huge combines going through the fields cutting grain, I always think of the way we used to thresh. We used a machine called a binder that cut the whole stocks of grain and made them into bundles. Then we made these bundles into piles or shocks that later we loaded by hand on to wagons pulled by horses and hauled to a threshing machine. This machine moved from field to field and was powered by a tractor. We loaded the shocks by hand on to wagons pulled by horses. The bundles were hand pitched into this machine, which separated the grain from the straw. The straw blew into a large pile to use for the animals bedding. We put the grain into bags, wagons or trucks.

I was a small boy when the threshing crew came to our field. I was excited about the great event of seeing men, horses and machines at work. My mother told me that I might go stand by the fence and watch. However, I was not to go near where the men were working. After the men loaded the first wagon, the driver started for the threshing machine. The noise and moving parts of the machine scared the team and they started to run. When the driver fell off the wagon, those ponies really began running. One of the men pitching bundles on the wagon in the field was half-Indian, and could out run any man in our valley even though he was over 50 years old. When he saw the team start running, he started running as well. He grabbed the back rack of the wagon, climbed on and across to the front of the wagon. From there, he jumped on to one of the horse's backs grabbing the lines and bringing them under control. From there, he drove them to the threshing machine to be unloaded. He continued to ride the horse controlling the other one for several loads until they became used to the noise and would stand while the wagon was being unloaded.

That Old Indian never ran in any marathon; he just ran for fun. We should enjoy life like the Old Indian. Approach every task with enthusiasm. Be happy and give your best effort.

HAYING TIME

"My first job." "As a seven year old I became stacker boy."

Today when its haying time, we take a big machine that has a sickle bar that cuts a 15 foot wide swath. Then the hay goes in an auger that takes it through a roller, putting the hay in a straight row behind the machine as it goes by. Then we come along with a big fancy baler.

We sit in our tractors with air conditioners that make it nice and cool. After we roll the hay into ton bales, we take the same tractors and stack the big round bales in long rows. In the winter, we turn the heat on in the cab of our tractor and put the bales in feeders. One man can do what 30 men used to do in the field.

We used to have mowing machines pulled by horses. There would be one man and two horses with each machine. We'd probably have six or seven of these machines going at the same time. These mowing machines only had five to seven foot cutting bars and they would mow only as fast as the horses could walk. Then a dump rake would rake the hay into long, straight, neat rows.

It was really hard work. We pushed the hay in with what we called a sweep rake, or a bull rake, or a buck rake, and it had big teeth. The horses got behind it or beside it and pulled. Then, hay would roll up into a pile. Then they would push it up on what they called a slide stacker or an overshot stacker. The team of horses would pull a cable that ran through pulleys making the head go up to the stack. Then anywhere from 4-6 men spread the hay around to shape the stack. When finished, the hay stack looked like a loaf of bread, with rounded tops and sloping sides, so the water would run off. They were about 20 feet wide and would be about 30 feet high.

We started haying after the 4th of July celebration and wouldn't finish until snow flew. It was a big operation. Sometimes we would have as many as 30 men working in the hay field, and we had 50-100 horses. We always had to have spare horses to keep from overworking our teams.

I was a little boy about seven and had to cut across the hay field to another field to irrigate. As I started across the field, I started watching the hay crew start a new stack. The boy driving the stacker team to pull the hay up to the stack wasn't much of a driver. He was lazy and undependable. He stopped the horses too quick and the hay would fall down in the stacker so the men would have to dig it out, or he'd go too hard and throw it clear over the stack. The men would have to pick it up with the bull rake and push it around.

The men became angry so one of them started driving the stacker team. The boy went and sat down under a tree in the shade. He was pouting and angry. He was going to quit because he wasn't getting enough money. He was complaining royally because he couldn't do the job. If he would have applied himself and paid attention, he could have learned. He was 15 and I was only 7, but I could see what the job needed.

As a small child, I rode the feed wagons in the winter to be out of my mother's way in the house or just to have something to do. I would hang over the front of the feed rack and would drive the team.

I knew I could drive that team of horses on the stacker because at home I pulled the stacker for my father. I kept everything out from under the head so it could lie flat down on the ground. I kept it raked up nice and clean. Also, I kept all the pulleys oiled. I had an oil can and took my job very seriously.

As I stood there watching, time flew by. All of a sudden I realized that I had been there longer than I should have when somebody grabbed me by the shoulders and said, "What are you doing here? Have you changed the irrigation water?" I looked up and it was my mother.

About then the owner of the ranch said to my mother, "Would you let this boy drive the stacker horses?"

Mother said, "It's all right if he can do it."

The rancher replied, "We'll see."

So I took the lines from the man that was driving the horses, popped the horses with the end of the lines and up we went. The hay landed in the middle of the stack. Of course, the men bragged on me, I felt ten feet tall, as big as any of them. While I was waiting for the next load to get on the head, so I could pull it up, I heard my mother say, "Well for a dollar a day, yes, he could have me."

By then I showed them I could put the hay where they wanted it. I carefully watched and listened to what they were trying to tell the stacker boy. If we watch very carefully, friends, we don't have to be shown or told. God gave us good brains, he gave us good eyes and if we will just watch, think and concentrate, we can see what's going

Runaway. "They shore tore up dad's new hay rake."

on. If the other person can do it, we can too. We can learn if we are willing to pay attention.

So, I started my first job at the age of seven. We went to work at 7:00 in the morning, then to the ranch house at 11:30 where we'd put our horses in the barn and grain them so they rested while we ate our dinner. At 1:00, we got them out and went back to the hay field, working until dark.

Sometimes my father worked there too. He ran one of the three bull rakes. They had four men on the stack, but after I started driving the stacker team they put six men on the stack. Instead of finishing one stack in a day, we were getting two full stacks, which was about 80 tons of hay a day. It was really a record. Nobody had to dig hay out of the stacker and that saved a lot of time.

From this time on I always had a job. Three years later I was riding the dump rake. When I was 13, I got to go on the stack. The stacker boy got paid a dollar a day. On the mowing machine he got $2.50 a day and on the stack you would make $10 per day. Those were good wages during World War II.

I thought I was getting to be a man. My dad and a neighbor thought so too. The neighbor was too old to take care of his ranch, so he rented me his hay fields. Boy, was I in the big time! Dad decided to buy a brand new dump rake, which made windrows of hay. It was a very expensive machine.

Well, the first cutting of hay was a fine crop. I had irrigated and done everything just right. I had a big stack of hay to show for my work and, of course this made me feel BIG!

When it came time to cut the second cutting, one horse in each of our two teams had a problem. One was lame and the other one was sick. Horses that always work together as a team do not like to work with any other horse. The two horses that were able to work both worked on the right side of the team.

Father told me which horse to put on the left side so that they would behave, so when I mowed, that is exactly what I did. When it came time to rake, I decided, that I would teach the other horse to work on the left side. Boy, what a mistake that was!

With much difficulty, I got them hooked up. If I had been smart instead of a "know-it-all," I would have seen all the trouble that was going to take place. They kept trying to turn around and get the way they should be.

We worked about two hours and had been having many problems when all of a sudden, they squealed, touched noses and started to run. No matter how hard I pulled on the lines, they just ran harder. I looked up to see we were heading for the hay stacker. That's when I jumped off the back of the rake. I hung on to the lines and went bouncing like a basketball, until I wised up and let loose.

As they went by the stacker, one rake wheel caught a corner of the stacker, breaking the rake all to pieces as well as wrecking the stacker. Also, the harness broke making those horses run all the harder. They were still hooked together by the neck yoke, and as they came to a fence, one jumped over but one did not. They ran another half mile breaking every post. When they reached the corner they stopped.

I thought I knew better than my father, but it ruined a brand new dump rake. We fixed it the best we could, but it never worked right again. It ruined half a mile of brand new highway fence and wrecked the hay stacker.

I sure was humbled when we figured up the cost. It took all the money I made from the piece of ground I rented that summer to pay for the mess.

Today, I am an old man but I have never been out of work, because whatever I do, I take it seriously. You know the Bible says, "whatsoever the hand findeth to do, do it with all thy might." Ecclesiastes 9:10 That means to do it to the best of our ability. Never be satisfied with the job you do. Maybe other people will give you praise, but somewhere in the job you'll see something that wasn't quite perfect. Don't beat yourself to death. Just look at it and say, "Now I could have done a better job, so if I do it again, I'll make sure I do it better the next time."

WINTER SPORTS

Dad always had fun pulling us. We shore would fly across the fields.

I sometimes think of the fun my sisters and I had when our father pulled us on our coasting sled behind his saddle horse when, the snow lay smooth and deep in the hay meadows. He would hook a long rope from the saddle horn to the sled. Then my sister and I would get on the sled. Away we would go as fast as the horse could run. Sometimes the sled would turn over and we would fall off into the deep snow. Dad would laugh and have such fun and so would we. It may seem like a very simple thing, but it was a time that a father could spend playing with his children. Besides sledding, ice skating was also part of our winter fun. We never had TV or radio so we made up our own fun.

In the summer, we went fishing, hiking, picnicking and horseback riding. I still enjoy the same winter sport, but now I ride the horse and pull my grandchildren on the sled. God tells us to be still and we will know him. If we will sit quietly, many times we will understand what to do for ourselves and others.

HAULING DRINKING WATER

"Ole Babe was shore old and tired, but was good to a boy like me."

When I was a young man, there was no electricity in our valley or even our town. The nearest electricity was 30 miles from where we lived.

My father organized the men of the community to begin the work for a power line. They dug the holes for the poles and strung the wire. All that we needed was for the electric company to hook it up.

Before we had electricity, we had no way to get drinking water except to carry it in from the river. Some people had a spring or a well, but my family got our water from the beautiful Colorado River. It was bright, bubbly and crystal clear. It was good water then because there was no pollution.

To bring the water from the river, my father made a little sled using two poles. He would then harness up our old mare named Babe who was very gentle and hook her to the sled. When she was younger she was a good "ole" work horse, but by then she was too old to work with the other horses. She was so gentle that as a little boy even I could harness her up. I would put two empty 50 gallon barrels on the sled and we would go down to the river.

Once we were at the river, I would take off my shoes, wade in and reach way out so I could get a half bucket of the clear water. Then I'd carry it and pour it into one of the barrels. It took most of the morning to fill both barrels. By carrying a bucket with two gallons of water in it, it took about 50 trips up and down the bank.

While the filling was going on, that faithful horse just stood there in the sun and slept. She was old and bony with bad teeth. After our barrels were full, I would cover them, and we would take off. She would pull a little way and rest, then she'd go until she tired again. When we got to the house, we pulled up to the back door where I would unhook that "ole" horse and turn her back out in the pasture with the calves.

"Ole" Babe was such a good horse who was so kind to me, and I was kind to her. I have memories of the many gentle horses and cows that I knew as a child and I think of how much fun it will be when we get to heaven and can sit by a bear or hug a lion. How we will enjoy all the great animals God has created for us.

"The cow and the bear shall graze. Their young ones shall lie down together. They shall not hurt nor destroy." Isaiah 11:7,9

"OLE" TOBY

"The best dog ever."

Old Toby was the first dog I remember. He was a little black dog with a white collar, similar to a border collie, but yet different. In the West, there were many of these types and we called them sheep dogs. They were very intelligent and loyal. The could work cattle, horses and sheep. They seemed to almost think like a man.

A sheepherder could take this type of dog and go out with several thousand head of sheep, wave his arm and by calling these dogs could move and take care of this large number of sheep. I remember seeing one cowboy taking many cattle down the road with these dogs running along beside the herd. If there was an open gate, or if there was a side road, they would sit in it and not let the cattle turn in.

Old Toby was one of these dogs. When it came milking time, he would go to the pasture and get the old milk cow or you could send him out to bring in the horses. He was a dog who lived outside, but let there be some shooting or a storm come up and he wanted in the house. When he came running in, you better look out because he would run right under a bed and you couldn't get him out until the storm was over.

Toby had only one bad habit, he loved to chase rabbits. Toby had all the food he needed. He was slick and fat and didn't need to chase rabbits. It was an especially bad habit for a cow dog because if a rabbit happened by while Toby was watching the gate, he forgot about watching the gate and took off after the rabbit.

I can remember strangers coming and Toby standing between the stranger and me snarling. He wouldn't let them get close. There was an irrigation canal on our ranch and as a little boy I thought it was such a big canal. It was about eight feet wide. At the deepest spot, it was about three feet deep. My father put a plank across the canal from where my older sisters and I would run out on this plank and jump in, yelling "help!" Toby would come running, jump in and grab us by our swimming suits and drag us to the shore. This was a lot of fun until mother found out what we were doing. She scolded us and made us quit because Toby was seriously rescuing us and we were making fun. Toby was a good guard dog and considered protecting us his responsibility. The only time when Toby wouldn't chase a rabbit was when he was watching over us.

One day Father took a wagon over to another ranch to get a load of hay. He was coming home along the road and Toby was trotting under the wagon. As they neared the spot where they had to cross the highway, Toby saw this big old jackrabbit run in front of the horses. Toby took off after him just as hard as he could go. When Toby ran after rabbits, he saw nothing but the rabbit. The rabbit headed across the highway with Toby right on his heels just as a car came along and that was the end of poor old Toby.

I was a very sad boy for a long time. I went where we buried Toby, sat down and cried because I had lost a very dear friend.

There are many people that let bad habits destroy their lives just as Toby's bad habit destroyed him. People become hooked on drugs, alcohol or tobacco, which take over their lives and eventually can kill them. If you are tempted to start one of these habits remember what happened to Toby.

"OLE" PEACHES

"She would put her head down for me to get on." "the cowboys would pay to see her do it."

I shall never forget the little bay mustang mare that was my friend and companion when I was a boy. It was Peaches who taught me to ride. She was my faithful little cowpony and friend.

My friends and I would gather under the bridge that crossed the Colorado river to go swimming. I always turned Peaches loose because she liked to play in the river just as much as we did. She would run and jump in the water and swim right along the side of all us boys. Sometimes she would take her head and push us under the water. She would even dive off the bank with us hanging on her back. Sometimes if you climbed on her back while swimming, she would roll over to give you a good ducking. None of the other boy's ponies would even get near the river let alone come in and swim with them. When my sister Mary Ellen rode her, Peaches would lie down in the water when ever they crossed a creek or the irrigation canal.

Shoeing the cow pony. "That ole pony would shore work hard." "She was the first horse I shoed."

Every fall we rounded the cows up off the mountain and drove them to the shipping yards. Then we loaded them in boxcars and shipped them to market. The ranchers would hire me to help drive the cattle across the valley lanes to our house, where the drovers stopped the herd for the night. In the morning, I would saddle Peaches and help get the cattle to the shipping yards and on the train.

Peaches was sure a good cowpony. She could out run any horse I ever came up against. We proved it many times in races. I had to keep quiet about it at home because I was not supposed to race since it could make a horse "run crazy." A horse that is raced too much can get so that is all they want to do and aren't good for anything else. She was lightning quick and could turn on a dime. That mare dumped me many times when she was turning a cow. I always knew when she was going to turn, but she was so quick that no matter how hard I tried to stay on it was good bye. When she got the critter straightened out, she always came back to me.

A young woman broke Peaches to the saddle, but she sold the horse when she came down with Polio, which crippled her so she was no longer able to ride. A short time later, my father bought the little mare and her colt for 20 dollars. Peaches loved woman and children.

If she wanted to, she could buck as hard as any mustang. With me, it always seemed as she was just teaching me to ride because she never bucked hard enough to dump me.

While she loved children and women, Peaches hated most men. Although she would work hard for a man who was good with horses such as my father, who was one of the best horsemen I have ever seen (and I have seen a lot). Though she would work for my father, it was evident that she did not like him. The pasture where we kept her was along the river and when my father went to catch her, Peaches would swim the river and take off until he left with another horse. When I went catch her, she always came to me.

There was a brand inspector that always used her at the shipping pens and she seemed to like him. Like Father, he was very good with horses. I helped get the cattle penned and then when I left to go on to school, the brand inspector used Peaches to sort through the cattle and check the brands. When he finished with "Ole" Peaches, he took the bridle off and hung it on the saddle horn. She then took off for home on a lope. If the gate to our lane was closed, she would whinny until Mother went and let her in. She always went right to the barn so we could unsaddle her.

In the spring when the cows were having their baby calves, we had to shut Peaches up because she drove the mother cows away from their calves and tried to mother them. When we moved cows and calves she went along watching for tired little calves who would lie down. She tried to get the calf moving again. If she couldn't, she stood beside it, waiting for us to come and help. If not for Peaches, we would have lost many calves.

When I first got Peaches, I did not have a saddle. I taught her to lower her head so I could hang on and be lifted when she raised her head. I taught her to do this by feeding her oats, which I always carried in my pockets. Many times the cowboys paid to see me get on this way. As I ran to her, she dropped the head down so I could jump a straddle of her neck. In a split second her head came up and off we went on a run. Sometimes I would still be sitting backwards. When a new hand came to our place, there was always betting that the kid could get on the horse while running. I always got paid well, but we never told Mother.

A year before I left home, my father got tired of Peaches swimming the river when he needed a horse, so he sold her to a man for sixty dollars. For a while I felt life was not worth living, until my uncle gave me the first quarter horse in our valley. I broke that pony to ride. He sure made a fine horse, but he never could match Peaches. I can't even remember his name.

The man that bought Peaches was a large cruel man. He fed her well, but beat her and jerked her around in a very cruel manner. That smart little horse just took his abuse until she got a chance to get even. One day the man started beating her and then gave a very hard vicious yank on the reins, which was more than "Ole" Peaches could take. When she felt the bit dig into her mouth, she reared right over backwards crushing the cruel man.

The saddle the cruel man used had a small steel horn that was quite long. When Peaches got back on her feet, the horn stuck in the man's ribs and he hung on the saddle. To punish him more, Peaches ran the half mile home, not stopping until she reached the yard gate. Then she whinnied for the wife to come. The only way the wife could get the man off was to cut the ladigo and let him and the saddle fall to the ground. He was in the hospital for many months, but finally got well.

While the man was still unconscious in the hospital, his wife sold Peaches to an old man named Phil, who had worked on ranches mostly breaking wild horses. This is where I saw her last. Phil was helping move cattle. He had two canes tied on the saddle. When old Phil died, the ranch owner gave the instructions that the "Ole" bay mare could have the run of his place and only little children could ride her. She died a very old and happy horse.

Be kind to animals and they will return it with rewards that cannot be measured.

“OLE” SCARNECK

Irigating. “We set the water about sun up.” “We used a colt and got them started.”

As a boy, I looked at the fine young mustang saddle mare named Peaches who my friend Buddy had and wished I owned that fine animal. My friend Buddy was very cruel to this horse. He did not love her as I would. I often talked to my Father and other men I worked for about how Buddy treated the mare. The answer was always the same, “She’s his horse; he owns her and it’s no ones business how he treats her.” That did not stop the hurt inside me when I saw her or even thought of her.

A couple of miles east in the hills ran a few bands of wild horses. The summer before, Peaches got out and went to the hills. She ran with a band of wild horses for a week or so before she came home. The next spring, the little mare gave birth to a fine colt. This was more than I could stand, "my" horse and a new colt.

Finally, my father went and talked to Buddy and his father and bought that wonderful bay mare and colt for twenty dollars, which was a very good price for those times. NOW I WAS KING! We fed the mare and colt very well. Dad put a sack of tobacco on her oats and that took care of the worms. It was not long until her ribs and bones did not show. She fattened up and got real slick and of course the colt grew like a weed. I was a real cowboy now with my own horse.

One day the world came crashing down around me because my uncle and cousin stopped to see us and the cousin saw my colt. I don't remember even naming that colt. My uncle offered Dad forty dollars for him and he sure owned that colt. They came and took him to their ranch one day while I was at school, which made it a lot easier.

In the West, we branded a horse as a colt, but we never used them before they were three or four. We let them run loose on the mountain. The summer he was three, my cousin Dick started to ride him to irrigate the hay fields every morning. When we saw Dick, he was full of wonderful stories of that great colt. He told of his first saddling and all the rest. He always ended up by saying, "There's no buck in that colt."

That fall they finished the roundup at the ranch in Milk Creek Basin (that was one of their three ranches). They turned most all the horses out into Axle Basin to winter out, which was the common practice then. When spring roundup came for the horses, which started earlier than the cow roundup, the horses were fat and looked good, especially the Colt. Now he would not let any person near him and could out run the mounted horses. They drove the herd and the colt thirty miles to the main ranch on White

River, the old TI headquarters.

The Colt was still very wild after a week, so Dick and some other cowboys ran him and some other horses into the main corral. With quite a lot of work, they got about a half dozen in the round breaking corral where it was easy to rope, snub up, halter and tie to the fence. The Colt was the last one caught and when the rope settled around his neck he sure went insane. They finally brought him under control, haltered him and tied him up. One could see the hate and rage in that pony. They left the colt in the breaking corral several days, with a long rope dragging from his halter to make it easier to catch him. He fought so hard when they roped him that the rope burned the hair on his neck, so that when it healed there would always be a scar on his neck.

When Dick went to saddle him that spring, he had to tie a hind leg up so that he could get up to saddle him. When Dick was on and seated, they untied the colt. Oh, how that colt would buck, very furious and vicious. Each saddling filled him with more rage and determination. Dick sold him to a rodeo bucking horse supplier. For many years, "Ole" Scarneck made fools out of the best riders. I never heard of anyone who rode him to the gun.

Scarneck reminds me of some people I know. No matter how good a start they have, or how good they get treated, they become so filled with self pity and hate that their lives are lonely and wretched. If we look for something good each day, it is always there and if we look for bad and dwell on that, it is sure there too. Always look for the good and positive. Be a ray of sunshine.

COW CAMP

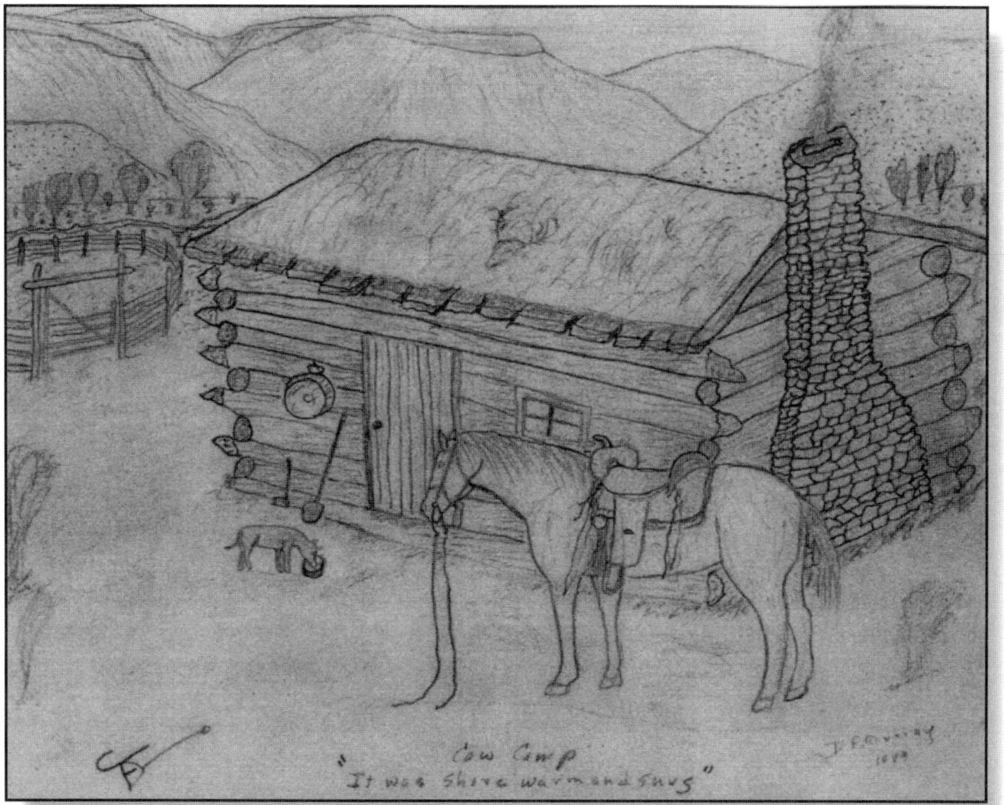

"It was shore warm and snug."

The cow camps in the Shale Oil Mountains of Western Colorado were very much the same as the ones in the picture at the beginning of this story. They built most of the cabins with aspen logs about eight inches thick. They most always had one or two windows about eighteen inches square with four panes. They made the doors out of one by ten inch boards. The roof had three large ridge logs length wise, one in the center and the other two on each side, spaced half way between the ridge log and side walls. Poles from two to three inches across lay over these or sometimes they used heavy boards. On top of this they laid brush covered by eight to twelve inches of dirt to act as insulation in the cool high mountains.

Inside, there was the old black cook stove with the water reservoir and tall warming oven. The stove pipe would go straight up through the roof. I remember cabins that were very old that still had fireplaces. They always used a cookstove in my time.

Across one end were the bunks, most generally a post fastened to the floor as well as the ceiling, about four feet by six feet with a board horizontally two feet above the floor, then another about thirty inches above the first one. A cowhide usually made up the bottom of the bed. They stretched the cowhide from the wall to the outer pole and then let it dry. We preferred cowhide or canvas over a bed spring and mattress, it sure made a fine place to put your war sack (bedding) and we doubled in the bunks when we slept. We always minded our manners, showing respect to the other fellow. Pegs were always very numerous on the log walls from which bridles, rope and personal belongings hung. Some had wood floors, which we considered very fancy and luxurious. The ones with dirt floors got moistened from time to time to keep them hard packed, so you could sweep them every day.

There was always a good wood table with enough chairs for each cowboy. Wooden grub boxes hung on the wall to keep food supplies. The grub box always contained a large supply of vegetables, potatoes, cans of tomatoes, green beans and corn. Gallon cans filled with rice, raisins, coffee, salt, sugar, and many types of dried fruit, peaches, apples, apricots, and prunes. Of course there was baking powder, pepper, nutmeg, cinnamon and other spices. There were larger tin cans, that held such things as flour, leftover biscuits, which were very good at any meal or anytime you were hungry. Also, there was the ten pound bucket of lard. A good cow outfit never fed their men sow belly and beans as TV and movies make out. We butchered fresh meat close to camp, generally deer, elk, or a yearling steer.

There was always a fenced horse pasture in which we kept the horses, the size of which depended on the number of horses the ranch owned. There was always a good round log corral about forty to fifty feet across with a large post set in the center about four and a half foot out of the ground. We used this pen to catch or start breaking horses to ride. It connected to a large rectangular corral made of poles fifteen feet long. It was more like a wall six feet tall with logs six to eight inches across. When it was possible, a stream ran through the corner, so the stock could always get water to drink.

About 3 o'clock, the cook would wake the horse wrangler, who generally was the newest and youngest cowboy. We kept the jingle or night horse in a small pasture along the creek, which was near the camp. Sometimes we kept this horse in a large corral. I have many times saddled one of these horses and headed for the far side of the large pasture. Range horses would usually start to move around 4 o'clock in the morning, so the wrangler needed to be on the back side of the herd by then. There was a bell mare who had a bell strapped around her neck so you could find the herd in the dark or in the brush. Sometimes you only got two or three clanks from the bell mare. If you did not hear the bell, you might do a lot of riding in the darkness to find the horses. After the nighthawk located them, he made sure he got on the opposite side of the herd, shouted, made noise, and then the fun would begin.

If the nighthawk let the herd walk, they spread out and only a small portion would get to camp. What a thrill it was bringing them into camp, jumping sage brush, washouts, streams, and dodging trees. I still get that feeling just telling it. When you were coming down the hill toward the camp, someone would always come out to shut the gate behind them. If no one shut the gate, the horses wheeled and stampeded out of the corral.

When I saw the lighted doorway, I always felt good because my job was over. When the corral gate closed and the night horse turned loose, it was time for breakfast, and what a meal! After washing your hands and face, breakfast would begin. Other cowboys got up, dressed, shaved, and whatever else they had to do, while the horse wrangler was running in the herd and the cook was cooking breakfast. Sometimes we had a regular cook, but most of the time a cowboy made the breakfast. Breakfast was a meal that was fit for a king! The meal consisted of steaks, biscuits, gravy, potatoes sliced and fried, some type of warm fruit sauce, and always plenty of strong coffee. The kids always got their cup, but it was always more water than coffee. We only ate lunch when we were close to camp. For supper we had meat, bread and potatoes with two vegetables. For dessert we ate fruit. On special occasions we had pie.

There was never any gossip and a man's personal things were safe as at home. The old time cowboy took pride in his appearance. He always tried to be neat and clean. Courtesy, cleanliness, and helpful consideration were always enforced or swift punishment would be meted out. This consisted of a good tongue lashing by one or all. In the most severe cases, they took the guilty one and held him face down across the back of a horse where they thrashed him with a pair of chaps. The ultimate was getting both a tongue lashing and a thrashing, and then getting fired. Firing was the prime insult to a cowboy.

I never knew of the cowboys sitting around the campfire singing songs and strumming a guitar. The main entertainment was the deck of cards, which they used to play poker. The man that bragged was not liked or accepted. The topics discussed were always the daily routine and its events. There were harmless pranks played on some poor unsuspecting soul but nothing dangerous because the work had enough risk for injury. We all worked to be the best at our trade. There was never any ridicule tolerated.

In our modern culture, we lose so much. I was lucky enough to see the very end of that life and we sure are the poorer because of its passing. The old time cowboys were very intelligent people, not at all like the dull ignorant reclusive person that Hollywood depicts today. They were tough, but could be kind and gentle to those in need. If we practiced the real old time cowboy's habits of honesty, hard work, courtesy, consideration, and helpfulness in today's world, it would make a much finer place to live.

THE OLD SCOT COWBOY

"To old and crippled to ride a horse."

"Ole" Reed was kind of an unusual looking man. I guess he was what we call a hunch back. His body was only around two feet long, but was great big around like a wash tub. If you measured him with a tape measure, he might have been five or six feet around. He had normal sized legs and a normal head, but his body was squished down into this short, big, round middle.

I used to work for "Ole" Reed. He and I would ride horses and move his cattle. He had a very strange idea. He said, "Cattle are worth $85.00 and horses are worth $15.00". Thus, when anyone worked for Reed they would eat horse meat instead of cow meat. Therefore most people didn't like to work for him.

After taking the cattle to the mountain, we headed back to the ranch. As we were coming off the mountain, a terrible wind storm came up. Even the rocks flew and rolled by us. Occasionally I'd hear him yell, and I'd look up to see what he was yelling about. I'd stop my horse just in time to see a rock or a piece of tree flying by me. Later he said to my father, "That boy was a gutsy little kid, why he kept riding no matter how bad it got. That kid never acted a bit scared. It was no different than if he was riding at a Sunday picnic." "Ole" Reed's praise made me feel big, but I had not felt so big and brave when we were out in the storm. I always thank the Lord for being there to watch over me during that storm.

Conn Mountain Trail. "Ole Reed and I came off the mountain in the worst wind storm that anyone could remember, it lasted four days."

TRAILING TO THE MOUNTAIN

"That ole cow shore was down, Tom and Norm said let her die." "I finally had to leave her." "I made a vow to always feed my animals."

I was nine years old when one of our neighbors who lived about ten miles from us saw my father in town and asked if I was busy as he needed help. It was time to take the cattle from the desert to the pastures in the high mountains where it was cool, the grass was good and there were no flies. Dad let me go.

This neighbor did not feed his cattle a mouth full of hay all winter. They just lived on grease wood, sagebrush and thistles. By spring, they were barely alive. They were skinny and so near death that their heads hung down and their bones rattled when they walked.

That first morning we got up at 3:00 A.M., saddled our horses and rode four miles to where the neighbor corralled the cows for the night without water or feed.

We started them moving when it was cool. They all had little calves on them. The neighbor had already branded the calves so they were ready for us to turn them out for the summer. We had this steep mountain trail to go up, which climbed 1,500 feet in two and a half miles.

This particular trail was on the south and west side of the mountain and it was bare. By ten o'clock the sun was beating down on the bare rocks. There were times when it reached 120 degrees.

It was my job to bring up the strays or stragglers. The stronger ones were up ahead because they knew where we were going. The boss and the foreman were riding in front. There were old cows that would get weak and fall down. They would lie there and it was my job to get them up and bring them on. As we got about three quarters of the way up the trail, there was a rim of rock. It was probably 75-100 feet through. About half way through this rim was a spring. Some of the cows got to the spring and lay down. Once they lay down, they couldn't get back up so the boss went on and left them to die.

I felt extra sorry for this one particular old cow. She had a calf, which was skinny and hungry because its mama had no milk for it. It was about 11:30 and we lacked about 300 feet of getting to the spring. There was a little bit of shade there by the rim.

The old cow fell down. I got off my horse, twisted her tail and pulled her horns trying to get her up. Being a child, this upset me very much. The calf was hungry, the cow was lying there with her stomach gurgling and she was dying. Her eyes were rolling and her tongue lolled out. It was very sad. In my mind, it is as vivid as if it happened ten minutes ago. The picture of the calf trying to nurse the cow's udder when there was nothing there, and the sound of the calf's cry when it didn't get any milk. Finally the calf lay down and couldn't get up. I yelled at the men to help me. They yelled back, "Ah let her go, she's dying anyway. Get your gun and shoot her." I didn't have a gun; I was only a child, so I screamed and cried. The poor thing, I tried to get her up, but it seemed beyond hope. She was more dead than alive. I stood there, screaming at nothing, at the miles and miles of empty space in the desert mountains. I made a vow before God and man that if I owned an animal I would never starve it. If you came to my ranch, you would see that I have kept my vow. All my animals are fat and slick.

God is good to us. When he gives us an animal, we have a duty to take care of it. The Bible says, "The righteous man considers the life of his beast." It also says, "The tender mercies of the wicked are cruel."

ANGRY BULL

"The horse and I escaped without injury, but I rode away on the saddle horn."

As a kid, we had this big bull who did a good job, but like most bulls in our country, he had a mean streak in him. He would fight anybody or anything.

One day while my father and I were milking the cows, we heard this peculiar noise. My father said, "I don't like the sound of that," so he went out and there was my little 5 year old brother pinned in the corner of the corral by the bull. My brother had a board with a nail sticking out of it. My brother was poking the bull in the nose and face, trying to keep the bull from getting him. Dad grabbed a pitch fork and came to the rescue. If not for the stick, the bull would have killed my brother.

This bull was an exceptionally good bull and every one of the neighbors wanted calves from him. He was hard to keep in because he would tear down almost any fence. One day the bull got out and went to the neighbor's place. The neighbor told Father to leave the bull at his place for a while.

Holding off the Bull. "Ole Jim was shore workin on that bulls nose."

When it came time to bring the bull home, my father got in the old pickup and I was on my saddle horse Peaches. When we got to the neighbor's place, the bull was a little sour. He didn't want to move. We didn't dare go around him on foot because he would charge, so I rode in close, giving Peaches her head and hung on to the saddle horn, because I knew we were in for a fight. The bull charged us and Peaches jumped out of his way. He charged her two or three more times and each time we kept working toward the gate in the direction of home.

Soon the bull realized what we were doing and started back for the neighbor's herd as hard as he could go. Peaches took off to head him back. When Peaches got ahead of him and turned in front of the bull, he hooked Peaches with his head and flipped her up in the air. Somehow she landed on her feet, but when she did I came loose from the saddle. The saddle horn was about the size of a 50 cent piece and I landed a straddle of it. Peaches hit the ground running and the bull was right after us. He was so mad he chased us all the way home. Somehow along the way, I was able to get back in the saddle.

I've thought many times that if Peaches had not been able to land on her feet when the bull threw us in the air, Peaches and I would have been killed. If the fall wouldn't have gotten us, the bull would have. I thank God that he gave Peaches the speed and agility to protect us from that angry bull. The devil would love to snuff our lives out, but God sends his angels to protect us.

LIVING A LIE

Broken Arm. "That ole bull shore threw me high."

There were many nights during shipping time that our corrals were full of horses belonging to different ranchers. There could be a hundred or more horses and many thousands of cattle in the fields. Most of them were at our place. They would be at our place for a night or two; however long it took to get room in the stockyards for loading the cattle on the train.

I was growing up with all this going on and I would watch what the cowboys did. It was not long until I began to think as they did and want to do the things they did. One thing the cowboys did was ride any kind of animal, whether a horse, a bull or whatever, they would ride it no matter how ornery.

To be like the cowboys, all of us kids in the neighborhood would get together and ride the milk cow's calves or any horses that bucked. There was a big yearling who I rode several times. With my Mexican spurs that a cowboy gave me, I thought I was a great rider.

One crisp, cool, moonlight night in the fall just before Halloween, the kids all came over to play. We talked about things to do and before long we boys decided we wanted to ride calves.

The calves were big yearlings and two year olds. We ran the calves into the corral. Several of the boys tried this one good sized calf, but the calf sent them all flying. It was then my turn to try. The calf gave it his all, but I stayed with him no matter which way he twisted and spun. I was feeling real big because I was the only one who could ride this calf when all of a sudden he got tired and stopped dead still. I was ready for him to make another jump, so when he stopped, I kept going. I went flying over his head and the ground was coming up very fast so I stuck my left arm out to catch my fall. This was a mistake because as soon as I hit the ground a sharp pain shot through my arm. I can still remember just how it felt. I went to get up, but my arm wouldn't bend. When I looked down, my hand was where my elbow should be. The elbow bones had slipped side by side. The lower part of my elbow was up to my shoulder and my hand was up to the other end of the other bone.

Mother never wanted me to be a cowboy. She loved and respected the hands, but she never wanted us children to be breaking horses or riding calves. I was afraid I would be in trouble so my friends and I concocted this story of how I fell off the gate as I was climbing over.

It was about 9 o'clock in the evening when we went into the house to let my folks know what had happened. It was apparent that I needed attention and the hospital was thirty miles away. My arm hurt, but the cowboys and my father taught me that a man didn't show any sign of pain. If it hurt, you never let anybody know it, so I didn't.

They put me in the pickup and we started over the mountain. They call them four wheel drive roads today, but then they were just wagon roads. We got to the hospital and after the doctor looked at it, he said, "We can set it, but do you want it straight or in a crooked position? If we set it back, the arm will always be stiff." After thinking about it, we decided to put it where it would be just about half way up, at a 45 degree angle. The doctor told me my arm would always be crooked.

I stayed in the hospital a day or two and then my folks came and took me home. They never asked questions about what happened. I'd told them I fell off the gate and that was the end of it.

After about six weeks, I went back to the doctor and he took the cast off, revealing this pitiful, shriveled weak arm. It was at a 45 degree angle, just a square corner and that was it. I could wiggle my hand, but my elbow wouldn't move.

A few months later, a horse got loose that had been tied with a halter rope. I jumped on my saddle horse and went after him. When I caught up with him, I grabbed the loose rope with my bad arm. When I grabbed the rope, this old horse spooked and yanked real hard. I heard something pop and I could move my arm. Once I could move my arm, I began exercising it and over time it pretty well straightened out. Over the years I have been able to use it, but it has been a constant reminder of the lie that I lived.

I didn't tell my mother what really happened until I had a wife and son that was already in school. What a relief it was to tell the truth.

It is much easier to tell the truth, even if we do get punished. It's still better than living a lie. Jesus is always willing to forgive us. If you have done something you are hiding, if you ask for Jesus to forgive you, and go to the person you lied to; you will feel better.

CATTLE ON THE ICE

Winter Tradgedy. "The herd fell thru the ice looking for water. As fast as they were roped we drug them out. The loss was small, that saved bankruptcy."

One cold winter day after we finished the morning feeding, we sat in the house warming ourselves beside the fire. In those days we did not have dial telephones. When you wanted to call someone, you turned a crank on the wall telephone, reaching the operator who then rang whoever you asked for. There were as many as 20 phones on one line, so the ladies of the community spent many hours listening to the conversations that went over the wires. When they heard the phone ring, they would run and listen to the conversations. We called this, "rubbering in." As we were warming up, the phone rang the distress call that was three long rings and two short rings.

My mother hurried to answer the phone and was told that a neighbor's herd of cattle had fallen through the ice into the river. Some local men driving trucks had seen the cattle on the ice when they had fallen through. They stopped at the ranch house to tell the people that their cattle were in the river. That is when they called for help. My father and I were some of the first to arrive. We brought horses and ropes with which to pull the cattle from the river. There were about 250 head of cattle in the water. Men that were good ropers went on the ice to rope the cattle. Those on horses pulled them from the river to the bank. We worked hard and soon had the cattle out.

Why were the cattle on the ice? In the winter, they cut a hole in the ice for the cattle to drink from. However that day no hole was cut in the ice. The hired man was angry that morning so he didn't cut the hole. In the middle of feeding, he decided to quit and go to town to get drunk. When the cattle became thirsty, they went looking for water. There was a place in the middle of the river that wasn't frozen so they started for that place to get a drink. When the ice broke, they all fell into the water. The owner of the ranch was out in the desert mountains looking after other cattle he owned. The next morning, my father and some other neighbors fed the cattle and cut a water hole while someone went to find the owner.

We always knew that if we needed help, our neighbors would be there to do whatever they could. That day we helped to save a man from bankruptcy, there was some loss among the cattle, but it was small. Without the neighbors responding to that distress call, all the cattle would have been lost.

CUTTING FENCE POSTS

"The skid hit a rock, the chain broke and I thought the team and Dad would be killed."

When I was 11, my father and I started going into the mountains to cut fence posts. We would take our team and wagon along with our lunch and sharp axes. When we reached the place to cut posts, we would look for the straight Juniper trees that would make eight to ten foot posts. Father would chop the tree down and I would trim the brush off. Then Dad would cut them to the right length. After we had several posts cut, we piled up 8 or 10, put a chain around them and drug them down the mountain side to where we left the wagon.

A wagon load would consist of about 30 posts. My father got a permit to cut posts from the forest service or Bureau of Land Management. They let us cut 100 posts every year, which usually took three to four days of hard work.

I remember one beautiful morning in particular. The sun was shining and the birds were singing and squaking. They consisted mostly of Blue Jays or Pinion Squakers as the old timers called them. As we arrived in the valley where we were going to leave our wagon, I remember the buzzards circling overhead and a band of wild horses that seemed to be curious about our team. We unhooked our wagon and started up the mountain side with our team and axes. We soon found a stand of trees high up on a little bench that were just right for making fence posts. We soon had a couple of wagon loads cut and ready to take down the mountain. The place where we were taking the posts down the side of the mountain was a little washout that kept the posts from sliding around and creating problems on the steep mountain side.

After we had taken several skids down, the dirt was wearing away from the rocks. There was one rock near the top that had a sharp point, which the chain caught on and broke. The posts flew in the air, landing all around Dad and the horses. When Father saw the chain break, he yelled at the horses to run and they and Dad started to run down the side of the mountain. Posts were falling around them and sliding as fast as they were running. They soon reached the bottom and stopped. When I saw this happen, I started running down the mountain with the axe in my hand. I tripped on the way down so the axe and I slid to the bottom just like the logs. The first thing I said when I reached the bottom was, "Are you Hurt?" Father's face was as white as a sheet. "I am all right but I thought we were going to be killed." I thought the same thing.

No matter what the situation we may find ourselves in, God is always there to watch over and protect us.

LITTLE COCK-A-DOODLE

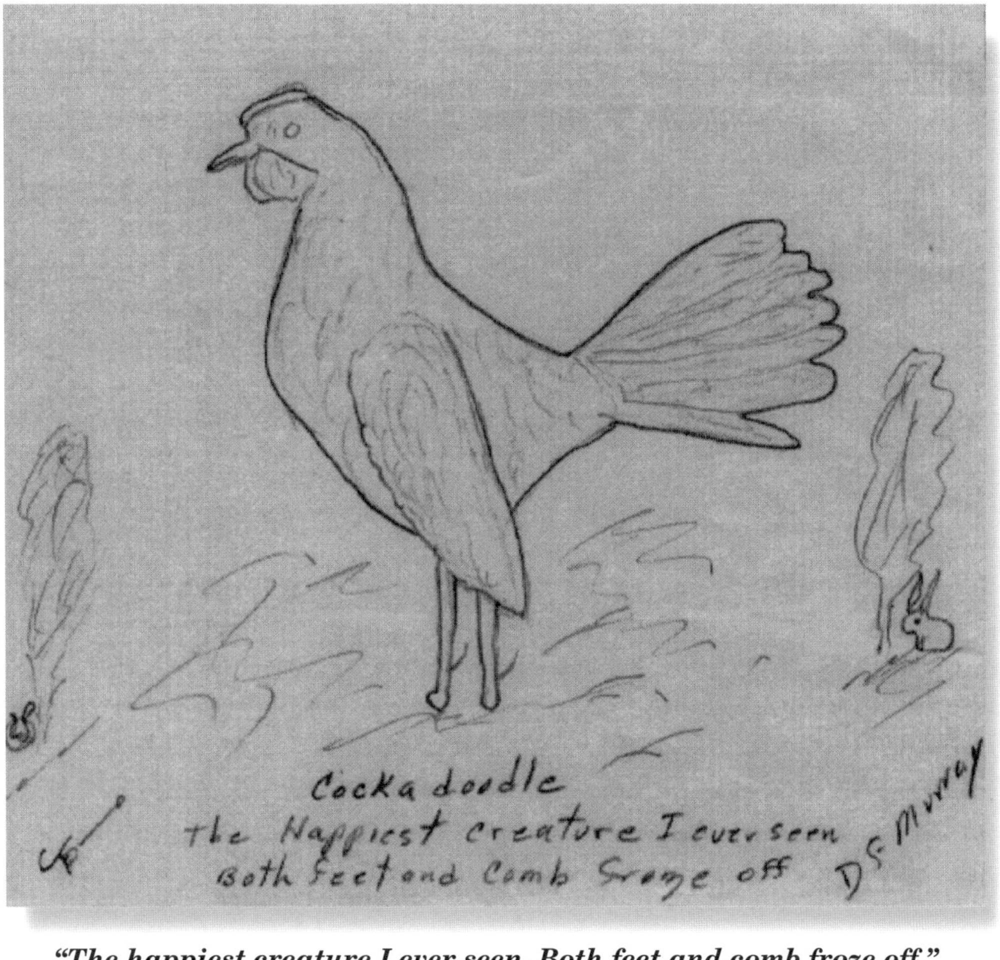

"The happiest creature I ever seen. Both feet and comb froze off."

On my farm where we break horses, we had a bunch of Banty chickens, two roosters, one black and a pretty red and yellow one along with eight little hens. They would go in the barn and would scratch in the stalls among the young horses. We had one little hen that would even fly up on their backs, pecking flies and other things. The horses became so used to this that when you were riding them out in the pasture they wouldn't shy when a pheasant flew up. They became so used to having something flap, flutter and make noise under their feet that they didn't pay any attention.

Winter came and it was about 20 below zero with a wind chill of about 75 below one night. When the barn is full of horses their body heat warms up the barn. It was very cold in the barn as well because we had only two horses left. My wife went to the barn to do the chores. When she walked in the rest of the chickens flew off the roost, but Cock-A-Doodle, the little red and yellow rooster, remained on the roost. When she went over to see why he didn't fly off the roost, she picked him up and found his feet frozen. One foot was completely frozen off and just the bone was there. On the other foot, all the toes were gone.

My wife always says, "Animals enjoy living." She is a person that loves all the little creatures God gives us. She put Cock-A-Doodle in a warm box and cared for him until his feet healed.

In the spring I noticed that Cock-A-Doodle would find something, but he couldn't scratch. He was always standing on the leg that had a foot. The one with the bone, he used as a kind of crutch just to hop along. When he found something he would call and call, and then one little hen would come. She would scratch for Cock-A-Doodle, and he got to eat before she did. Sometimes she would find some bugs and she would call him to come eat with her.

The bible tells me that God sees each little sparrow fall and it meets his tender view. I think if God loves those little creatures, I know he loves me too. Friends, every time I see Cock-A-Doodle and his little hen scratching for him, I know that God cares for me.

BITY MAN

Bronc Breaking. "That ole colt would go so high you thought he would never come down."

I stood at the corral and leaned against the fence, watching this beautiful two year old sorrel horse. It was a deep red sorrel horse with four stocking feet and a blaze down his face, the type of horse that any horseman appreciated. He would stand out in any crowd. He was a good sized colt and you could tell he was very athletic. He had the muscles to be a good cow horse, but also the beauty and conformation to be a show horse. He looked as if he would have the speed of a racehorse. The type of horse any person enjoys looking at.

While I was looking at him, the owner came. We went on about our business, but I couldn't keep my mind on what I was doing because I kept thinking about that pretty sorrel horse. There was something about his eyes that I had never seen in a horse. Now Range horses have a glassy, starey look like that of an outlaw. They don't look at anything in particular, but see everything. Then there are horses with soft eyes who usually are gentle. Some horses show fear in their eyes. This horse's eyes, I couldn't quite put my finger on what they looked like. I went ahead with my business and left.

I came back several more times during the summer. No matter what I was doing I always had to get a look at this horse. Finally, I said to the man, "how much will you take for that horse? Will you sell him?"

He looked at me, and said, "I gave $2,500 for him as a weanling." I did my mathematics and figured that the horse was now worth about $6,000. I decided right there that I would never be able to buy him.

In August just before Fair time, I stopped at the ranch to help them get the horses ready and he said to me, "Do you still want to buy that horse?" I knew I couldn't afford it so I turned him down.

It was Friday evening and the kids were all home from school for the weekend. We were sitting around talking when I heard a knock on the door. When I opened the door there stood this man and his daughter. He came in and asked me, "What would you charge me to get that big, tall colt ready to go to the National Western Stock Show in Denver."

The National Western Stock Show came about the first week in January. They have a very good horse sale and one of the best stock shows in the world. I knew that this horse was worth something and would bring a lot of money. Also, I noticed that whenever I asked about this horse, the man would get a panicky look in his eye, a look of fear. Because of this, I suspected there was something wrong with this horse so I told him that I would do it, but I quoted a much higher price than I normally charge. The man quickly agreed.

Just as they went out the door, I said, "I'm going to ship my cattle on Sunday so they will be at the auction for Monday's market. I'll be home about four o'clock so I will come over then and pick up the horse in my stock trailer."

The girl looked at me and said, "We can't, load him or tie him." They shut the door and left.

When I went to get the horse, I had the hired man along. The hired man was a good man, but he didn't know that much about livestock and sometimes he could do some foolish things.

When we got there, the man wasn't home, so I handed the girl the halter and lead rope and went out to the corral to get the horse. I had a hard time untying the rope that was around the gate because it had not been untied for a long time.

The girl went in, all the way across the corral toward the colt. She was going, "Whoa! Whoa! Whoa!" The further she went the faster she talked until she appeared terrified and had the horse scared as well. Somehow she got the halter on him.

As she started to lead him, I could see that her fear was upsetting the colt so I took him from her. I softly talked to the colt for about 5 minutes until he calmed down enough for me to lead him out of the gate. I led him to the trailer and we walked right in. As soon as we were in the trailer, the hired man slammed the door shut. I was lucky because the door didn't catch. If this horse had been an outlaw he could have killed me in the tight quarters of the trailer. When the colt realized the door was shut, he ran backward as hard as he could run to get out of the trailer. When he hit the gate, the gate popped open and out he went. I didn't let the rope get tight or try to hold him I just ran with him. When he stopped, I softly talked and petted him until I got him all calmed down.

While I was doing it, I asked the hired man why he had shut me in the gate. His excuse was that the girl told him that if he got out you would never get him in again. Well, I have yet to see the horse that can't be loaded in a trailer! So I made the man stay back while I lead the horse in and tied him in the trailer. Then I shut the center partition gate and the back door and we went home.

When I got home, my wife who loves animals came out to look at this pretty horse. She asked, "What's his name?" Well, I hadn't thought to ask the girl his name. To my wife, names are important. Now to me, an old cowboy, you don't worry about a horse's name. You just sort of put your own name on it.

Just about the time supper was over, several neighbors happened to stop by. One lady said to me, "Fred, do you have this sorrel horse that belongs to those people?"

I said, "yes."

She replied, "Oh, don't mess with him, he's an outlaw, he'll kill you."

Well, I've spoken out of turn many times. I was kind of like old Shake, when he said, "Blaze away, little lady, blaze away." I jokingly said, "Well I haven't been killed yet." which made her cry. I could see there was something more to the story.

She began to tell me how this horse had a saddle turned under him and how a fence that he had been tied to fell down and he dragged it through the neighbor's field, ruining the crop. When I got her calmed down, she told me the whole story or at least the part she knew. When they saddled the horse, the cinch wasn't tight. When the man went to get on, the saddle turned under his belly. He went to bucking and kicking until he tore the saddle completely off. I had seen a saddle lying in their garage all torn to pieces, but I never thought anything about it. It wasn't that unusual at a place with many horses.

Then she told me that they tied him to a wood fence that was not strong. Because he was afraid, he started pulling back, which tore the fence down. This really scared him and he started running, but couldn't get away from the fence. He drug the piece of fence all over.

People were running after him yelling, "Whoa, Whoa, Whoa!" This just scared him more. They didn't know what to do because the horse was loose. If you just stop and let him alone he will quiet down. Then you slowly and quietly walk up and catch him.

When everyone finally left, I went back to the corral with my wife. A horse trampled me one time so she made me promise that I wouldn't saddle a new horse or start a new horse without someone being there. We went to the corral and I hooked a spotlight on the fence rather than turn on all the lights. That way, if anybody went by, they wouldn't know I was there and come bother me. When I'm working with a horse, one distraction might mean disability or your life. Well, my wife learned a long time ago that she never made a noise when the horses were fighting and trying to get away. She just stood and watched.

I brought him out of the barn and tied him to a metal ring on the side of the barn. The side of the barn was smooth so horses wouldn't hurt themselves if they went to fighting. I tied him up with one hand and slipped the saddle on with the other. Now, you remember, they had said that this horse couldn't be tied. Well, I had tied him in the trailer and on the barn, besides having put the saddle on him.

Let's go back to when I led him from the trailer and put him in my barn. I put him in a stall. I always do this when I first get a horse to break. I put them in a stall and get a little pan of grain. Then, I sit on the manger, shaking it and let them come to me. I want them to depend on me for food because if they do, they will learn to trust me.

When I sat down on the manger he didn't want to come to me, but finally he came, took a bite of grain and ran to the back corner. My wife who was watching said, "That poor horse is afraid. he's really scared." A bit later she said, "He keeps looking at your cowboy hat," so I took it off and laid it outside the stall. Then he came right over and ate the grain. He was just as friendly as could be.

Now let's get back out to the side of the barn, I eased back, pulling the cinch up tight, and this poor horse came undone. Now he was tied up and couldn't get away. The poor thing bucked and jumped in place for 45 minutes. He threw himself and skinned his head up, it was really sad. If there would have been any way I could have cut him loose, I would have, but I couldn't get near enough. Finally he quit and I put him back in the stall.

The next night we did the same thing. It was late so I thought nobody would come around to bother me. I had just tied him up, put the saddle on him and he had started to buck when I heard a man's voice from behind the lights say, "Well Mary Ann, look there, he hasn't even tightened the rope up." I looked at the rope and sure enough he was bucking and jumping, but he wasn't pulling himself back or throwing himself as he had the night before. I walked over where I could see behind the light and there stood the deputy sheriff, a friend of mine who lived near by. He was on his patrol and saw the lights from the opposite hill. He came to watch what I was doing. He knew enough about horses that he walked up quietly. He never uttered a sound or did anything to distract me. When the horse stopped bucking, I put him in the barn.

The next night I took him out, tied him up and put the saddle on him. He didn't do a thing. He stood perfectly still. I got a long piece of baling twine and tied it to my stirrup, jerking it and making it flop up and down, but it didn't bother him at all. He just stood there. So I took a long rope and hooked it to the halter. I put the end of the rope in the middle of the corral where I needed to stand. Then I untied him from the barn, turned him loose and took hold of the end of the long rope.

He stood there for just an instant until he realized that he was free of the barn. He sat right back flat on his tail, then jumped as high as he could and went to bucking around the corral on the end of the rope. It was more like the way a deer bounces than a mean horse who lands very stiff and hard in a way that will jar your bones and can knock you loose if you are on their back. He didn't do that, he bounced very gracefully, round and round in a circle because I was holding him, making him go in a circle around this small corral that was about 40 feet across. In about 30 to 40 minutes he got tired and stopped bucking.

My corral slopes so the water will drain away and he was down the hill below me on this short slope when he stopped. He turned and faced me. He started toward me very slowly. When he did this, I quit talking and just looked at him. I could hear his heart beating and hear him breathing. His head was up high and his nostrils were flaring. He was making a snorting sound and the whites of his eyes were showing. The whites of his eyes were all red and I thought, "Is he going to take me?" I looked at him and started softly talking to him. When he came to within four feet of me, my wife said, "You better get your whip!" It was lying at my feet so without taking my eyes off him I took my foot and lifted it until I could grab it without bending over because that would have put me at a disadvantage. I just stood there with the whip in my hand. I didn't want to use it, but I had it just in case I might need it. All of a sudden he dropped his head, walked up and stuck it right under my arm. This was more than I could take. Friends, I am not ashamed to cry. They say that I cried a little bit that night. My wife wept too because it was so sad to see this great beautiful horse and realize that somebody had abused him.

The next night I took him out; he ran his circle and bucked. After he stopped, I got on and rode him. For many days, every time I saddled this horse, I would saddle him up, put him on the end of the rope and let him run to get his buck out before getting on him. This is one of the very few I ever did this with.

He bucked once with me and once with my son Joe. A horse always bucks the same way. They have a certain pattern. If you watch a horse buck and study it, you know exactly what their pattern is and then you can ride accordingly. Having watched him buck with the saddle on I was able to figure the pattern out, which made him very easy to ride. Besides he barely seemed to touch the ground when he bucked, which made it even easier.

The man who owned him came over one night after I had ridden the horse about 45 miles that day. I asked him, "Do you want to ride your horse?"

He said "Oh no," but I told him to come on out. I rode the horse a little bit there in the corral and then the man got on. He rode him a little bit, but I could see that the man was afraid. Then the man just happened to remember he forgot to tell me about the saddle turning under the horse and that he pulled the fence down among other things, but he never would tell me the whole story.

After Christmas, just before we were to take the horse to the sale at National Western, the owner came over just as I was going to one of my friend's house. We were going to have a trail ride. The weather was warm for that time of year, so I asked the man to go along. I put his horse in the trailer for him and we left.

When we arrived, I took his horse out and put his saddle on the colt. Then I rode him around for a few minutes to make sure the horse was calm. I got off and turned the horse over to the man. Everything started off fine. I was out in front with my friend and the man was riding behind with some other people.

We had gone about a half mile north from the farm house when one of the boys riding with us came up and said, "You should go back there, that horse is getting very excited." So I went back. The man was trembling and the horse was trembling, so I talked the man into getting off. I held the horse carefully while he got off and got on my horse. Then I worked the colt a little bit and he calmed right down.

On the way home, the man wanted to know If I wanted to buy the horse for $2,000. I said, "No, I wouldn't give you a $1,000." Now I wanted the horse, but this is all part of horse trading. You see, one man starts high and one man starts low and then you haggle back and forth. When we finished, I bought the horse for $1,200.

When spring came, there was a horse show in the little town about three miles away, so I took him and another horse. I didn't expect this horse to win, but I rode him. I wanted him to get used to the noise of a crowd. Although we didn't win, he worked beautifully.

In a few days his former owner came to my house and said, "They tell me you rode Bity Man at the horse show." When I told him that I had, he decided it was time to tell me the rest of the story. He had taken him to a trainer who got on Bity and started jerking on him, pulling him over backwards. Even though it was the trainer's fault, he brought the horse home because he thought the horse was worthless since he flopped over backwards.

Then, the man took Bity to a place by Omaha were they had four "cowboys" who broke horses. Bity kept bucking them off so they tied him in a hallway with a chain to each side of his halter. With a "cowboy" on each side, they took clubs and beat Bity until he couldn't stand up. They did this every day for two weeks. After he was able to get up from the beating, they would try to ride him, but they still fell off. So they gave up and brought him home. It was after this, that the saddle turning and fence incidents happened.

We use Bity on our ranch here all the time. He will do anything my son Joe or I want. If a stranger with a cowboy hat comes up even after all these years, he is still afraid of them. I will go out in the morning and I will say, "kiss me, Bity Man." He will take his lips and rub them all over my face. All I have to do is call and he will run from the pasture to see me.

I think of life. We mistrust people. We don't believe in people. We feel sorry for ourselves and we even hate people. If we let Jesus takes over, He will gentle us. He will teach us that he loves us, and that there are people that love us. So when you think about Bity, remember that Jesus is kind and gentle. He will give us a home in Heaven where nobody will ever abuse us again.

LEAVING TEXAS

"He borrowed the first horse he came to."

In 1954, I was a young man working on a cattle ranch in western Colorado. While there, I became acquainted with a man who was 96 years old. One day as we were visiting, he pulled up his pant leg and there were three black marks about two inches apart under the surface of the skin. He asked me, "Young man, do you have any idea what these are?"

To which I replied, "I don't have a clue what they are."

His answer was, "Well they are bullet slugs from a six shooter."

Lee went on to tell me the story of how he got the bullets in his leg. As a boy of 15, he thought he was as big and tough as any man that ever rode a horse. One day Lee and his brother went with friends to a saloon to get drunk. After drinking for some time, he decided that he was going to buy drinks for everyone, but there was one man sitting alone in the corner who said, "Thank you, but I drink alone."

This made Lee boiling mad. He took a bottle of whiskey and his six shooters to the table where the man was setting and said, "You will drink with me!"

The man politely said, "Leave me alone or you will be sorry." Lee laughed because he was holding his gun.

Before Lee knew what had happened, he was on the floor with the table upside down on his legs. The man stood over him with both six shooters drawn and said with a sneer, "I am going to count to three. If you are still in my sight, I will kill you!" Lee decided that he better haul freight in high fashion. As he went out the door he heard three shots and felt their sting in his leg.

Outside Lee grabbed the first horse he saw and swung on. That was the beginning of many "borrowed" horses that took him to Canada. He would take a horse and ride it until it got tired. Then he turned it loose, knowing that it would go back home.

When he reached Ogallala, Nebraska, his brother finally caught up with him. The first thing he said to Lee was "You little fool, you should have known better than to have drawn your gun on the best gun fighter in the whole state of Texas. He could have killed you in the blink of an eye."

After reaching Canada, they worked for cow outfits for several years. Then they started working their way south on roundups through Montana and Wyoming. After several years, they reached Northwestern Colorado, helping to bring some of the first herds of cattle to that country while the Indian wars were still occurring.

Lee would tell stories about the cowboys racing their cowponies against the Indians ponies. Whoever won got the other's horse. When the cowboys lost, they waited a few days and then told the army that the Indians stole their horses. With a great laugh, Lee told how the army went and retrieved the cowboys' horses from the Indians.

I don't know how long Lee lived because I left that part of the country soon after, but I do know how he spent his time. He walked four miles to town every morning to sit and visit with his old-time cowboy friends. He walked because he was too crippled to get on a horse. Early in the afternoon, Lee limped back home where he did some work around his place, made supper and went to bed.

Sometimes we get to thinking we are awful mighty and good. Remember, there is always somebody out there that is just a little bit better, a little bit faster, a little bit stronger than you are. So before you start bragging and telling how you are better than someone else, remember the three bullets in Lee's leg.

QUEEN ANN'S WAR

"She would rope, then dump and break their knecks, she was gettin even for the killing of Matt Rash."

Annie Bassett was born just after her folks came to Brown's Park from the East in the late 1870's or early 1880's. They came west to the dry climate and warmer winters of Brown's Park because of their health. When Annie was born, her mother was very sick and had no milk to nurse Ann. Her father knew that if the baby was to live, he must find someone to nurse the baby. An old outlaw named Joe Herrera volunteered to go to the Ute Indian camp and make a deal with an Indian woman to nurse the child. She came over 2-3 times a day and would hold this little white haired, blue eyed baby and nurse her.

Annie grew into an attractive and intelligent young woman. Her parents sent her back East to private school. She traveled in Europe and England. She had all the best things because her parents were hard working, successful people. Up on returning from the East, Annie was full of life and started dating a cowboy named Matt Rash who lived nearby. Matt and Annie fell in love. Before long, Matt asked Annie to marry him and she accepted his proposal.

Just east of Brown's Park, up on the flats across the Great Divide, was Ora Haley's giant Two Bars Ranch, which had over a 150,000 head of cattle covering an area of 150 miles. Haley wanted to crowd all the little ranches out. He wanted everything for himself.

Ora Haley, Hy Bernard and the other men who ran this ranch had more money than they knew what to do with, but they wanted more. They were never satisfied. Now, there is nothing wrong with making money, but when it becomes the only goal of your life and you resort to anything to get the next buck regardless of the consequences; it is wrong. This is what happened to the men of the Two Bars.

To get rid of the small ranchers, Ora Haley hired a killer by the name of Bob Meldron, who delighted in killing. Then Bob hired Tom Horn, who was the most notorious, vicious killer. Their job was to kill anybody who got in the way of the Two Bars interest.

Tom Horn would come into a country and hang around maybe six months to a year. He got to know the people he was going to kill by becoming their friend. He worked with them, whatever they did he went along. Once he earned their trust, he got them in a vulnerable position and then shot them down in cold blood, usually in the back. For doing this, his employers gave him good horses and a big wage, which was more than he could get doing honest work.

Horn spent several months in Brown's Park, getting to know all the people. He learned their daily habits such as when they got up, ate and went to bed. One morning he left the community, but a few days later he snuck back and hid in the sagebrush. Tom was ready to ambush one of the small ranches. As they came outside, he killed three of the men and Matt Rash was one of them.

Ann knew for sure that Ora Haley and Hy Bernard hired Tom Horn. She met Hy up on Douglas Mesa and threatened to kill him. It intrigued Hy that a young woman would stand up to him and he laughed at her. The way he laughed only made her more sure he was one of the men that hired Tom Horn.

Seeking revenge, Ann started a personal war against the Two Bars Cattle Company. If any of the Two Bars cattle got close to Brown's Park, she took Matt Rash's good sorrel rope horse and ran at the Two Bars cattle, which made them run away from her. As they ran, she took down her rope and roped one of the cows. Just as the rope tightened around the cows neck, she'd turn at a right angle, flipping the rope over the backside and when the cow hit the end of the 60 foot rope, it would flip, breaking its neck. If the jerk didn't break its neck, landing on its head would do the job.

If there was a large bunch of cattle, she drove them down across the Green river and down Ledore Canyon, then out onto Diamond Mountain. The Two Bars lost many cattle this way.

Over her lifetime, Ann became know as queen of the rustlers. Queen Ann got blamed for many things she didn't do, but there were many things she was guilty of doing. Just as greed destroyed the men of the Two Bars, the desire for revenge turned a beautiful young girl into a tough outlaw.

We live in a cruel world with many evil people who may do you wrong, but this is no excuse for you to do wrong yourself. Our prisons are filled with people who claim they have been wronged. "Everyone else is at fault." "It isn't fair." These excuses are never legitimate. We are responsible for our own actions. We must do what is right regardless of what others do.

SCHOOL MARM

Crossing the Green River. "The river was to high for wagons, so we loaded the cook stove on a good ole pack mare."

In early pioneer days, women, as young as 15 years old, could teach school if they could pass the teachers test. Young women, like Laura Ingalls Wilder in her "Little House" books, tell of the hard life these young but faithful teachers lived. These stories were repeated as many times as there were school houses.

The great blizzard of January 12, 1888, shows the great heroism of these strong willed young ladies. That blizzard was called the "schoolchildren blizzard" by many historians. These young teachers saved the lives of many of their students. My mother had a very good friend who was one of theses great pioneer ladies. I was fortunate to get to know her when I was a small boy. Winnie was her name.

In the days that Winnie taught school on the frontier, teachers were hard to find. When a teacher could be found, she was given board and room with someone in the community, usually parents of one of the students.

Many teachers gathered and cut the wood for the heating stove. They carried drinking water from a well, which sometimes could be as far as a half mile from the school house. In addition, many of them walked several miles to and from school, some days in knee deep snow. Marriage was usually the reason these fine ladies quit teaching school. Many times, there was no school because of the weather.

My father and many other people of his age owe a lot to these teachers who taught them readin', writin' and 'rithmatic, along with discipline and social graces.

My mother's friend Winnie could hold a person spellbound by her many stories of the pioneer days of school teaching. The story that stands out most in my mind is the one about moving day.

In Brown's Park the country is divided by the river. Then there were not any bridges. The only crossing was a ferry at the north end of the valley. A man named Albert Specks who had been a slave boy as a child in Georgia operated the ferry. The ferry did not operate when the river was frozen or flooding.

When the spring thaw came to the mighty Green River, it would be at full flood stage. Of course, this would not stop anyone in Brown's Park from crossing the river. They only spurred or whipped their saddle horse harder to force them into the river to swim across. They were wet and cold when they reached the other side. On arriving on the other side, they would make a large fire with which to dry out and warm up.

There was a school on each side of the river and there was a dirt roofed cabin on each side of the river, where the teacher lived during the school term. The teacher had to move every time she switched schools. While school was in session on one side, the children on the other side helped with the ranch work. Winnie taught both schools.

School ended on the east side and was ready to begin on the west side. This meant Winnie needed to move across the river. Unfortunately, the river was at full flood stage on the day the school marm planned to move. The wagons and ferry couldn't be used to move her because of the wild and raging water. Therefore some cowboys were going to help her move. They brought a string of good old gentle pack horses. Winnie rolled her belongings in a tarpaulin to keep them from getting wet. A cowboy lashed her belongs to the backs of the horses. Then the cowboys made the horses swim the river. One horse carried table, chairs and bedstead. Another horse carried groceries and cooking utensils. While, another carried clothing, books and personal belongings.

When it came time to move the cookstove, no one could figure out how to get it across the river because it was too big and cumbersome to carry on a saddle horse. After pondering the situation, a wise old rancher said, "Get me a big fat bellied horse because they are the best swimmers. The fat belly helps them to float."

Soon they found a fat old mare. They padded the old mare's back with plenty of saddle blankets, set the stove on her back and lashed it around her belly. A lariat was "dallied" on to each corner of the stove and to the saddle of four horses, which would help balance the stove. They lead the mare across the river with the cowboys on their horses swimming along side, using their ropes to balance the load. They unloaded the stove and set it up in the new home.

The students that went to those schools grew up and became good citizens because the obstacles that were placed before them were not allowed to stop them. Instead they found a way to overcome these obstacles with the guidance of their parents and teachers. Sometimes we see people today who give up and quit when a challenge arises. When it looks as if there is no way to get a job done or realize a dream, remember there is a way to accomplish that which is worthwhile. One of those great pioneer teachers, taught me as a small child when she was a very old lady. She had a saying that gives me great strength and courage. It goes like this, “If at first you don’t succeed try, try again.” Thank you Miss Thomas.

BOOTLEGGER'S CONFESSION

"And you that's hiding from the Lord." "Ole Franks life was shore different after that."

I had a friend named Frank who I used to work with. We'd ride horses to Dry Fork cow camp to round up cattle for the Latham Ranch. Frank, a religious man, read his Bible and prayed every day. We didn't go to the same church, but he would talk to me about the Lord. One day I said, "Frank have you always been a Christian?"

"Oh no Freddy, I was once a bootlegger."

In the 1920's and early 30's alcohol was illegal. There were men who sold illegal whiskey and if caught with it, they paid a fine and spent some time in prison. These people running whiskey would stick a bottle of it in their boot. When they found somebody to buy it, they pulled it out and sold it to that person who would stick it in their boot. This is how they became known as bootleggers.

Frank had a whiskey distillery about 20 miles outside town in a canyon in the wild country. Like many old time cowboys, Frank had no idea what made a car go, but he had enough money from selling whiskey that he bought a new 1933 Ford car. He hired a young fella in town, named Doug, to drive for him. They drove to the distillery and loaded the car up with fruit jars of whiskey. Then they took off to sell it. Frank carried two six-shooters and over his arm he carried a rifle.

One night when they neared town, they could see that the Federal men and the Revenuers had set up a roadblock and were waiting for them. Frank said to Doug, "Take off across the sagebrush and go around them." When he did, "Ole" Frank just opened the door and rolled out in the sagebrush while Doug went on.

When Doug got to the other side of town, the second roadblock caught him. They saw this 15 year old kid with a load of whiskey and knew it couldn't belong to him. They scared him, but he wouldn't talk. Finally, when they threatened to hang him, he said, "Yes someone was with me, and in the excitement of it all, he jumped out of the car." But he didn't tell them who it was.

When Frank jumped out of the car, he was near a revival meeting held in a tent on a vacant lot. He crawled through the sagebrush until he got to the tent. The tent was too long for the poles so they rolled and wadded up the extra canvas underneath. Frank crawled in under the folded canvas.

As he lay there hiding from the federal men, he could hear the preacher speaking and the federal men on the outside talking while they walked around. He heard one say, "I looked inside and he wasn't there," which made Frank breathe a sigh of relief.

They kept walking around and the preacher kept preaching about

Jesus. Frank had nothing else to do but to listen, and listen he did. "Pretty soon," he said, "the Lord touched my heart." Right then the old preacher said, "You that's hiding from the Lord, come forth!" Frank always waved his arm when he said that. He says, "I crawled out with my 30/30 across my arm and my six-gun at each side. I went to the altar and fell down on my knees, making my confession." In the middle of the confession, the preacher yelled very loudly, "All you saints come forward and pray!" Frank didn't know until later, but the preacher's reason for having all the people come and surround him was that he saw one of the Federal men looking in the tent door. One of the Federal men said, "Well he can't be in there, they're all praying."

That was the end of Frank's bootlegging days. He became a very fine Christian man. As the old saying goes, "The Lord works in mysterious ways." Frank is dead now, but I'm looking forward to seeing him in heaven some day.

WHISKEY RUNNING

"They killed the only good one of the outfit."

While it is nothing to brag about, Western Colorado and Eastern Utah were home to some of this nations most notorious outlaws. The most famous being Butch Cassidy. As sheriff of Vernal Utah, my grandfather tangled with many an outlaw during the 1890's and early 1900's. One of my most prized possession is a rifle given to my grandfather by the Governor of Utah.

The frontier had ended in most parts of the United States. However the rugged mountains and deserts of the area limited the amount of people who had settled in the region. The primary settlers were Mormons who had chosen the place in large part because they thought that no one else would want it. Everywhere else they settled; they had been subject to persecution. Therefore they hoped to be able to practice their religion as they saw fit. For the most part, they realized their dream. However, the Church changed their official view on polygamy in order for Utah to be granted statehood.

Unfortunately, while the rugged terrain and desert air provided a refuge for those who wished to have religious freedom, it proved to be a great haven for those who broke the law. For example, outlaws used the famous Robbers Roost as a hiding place because it was over 100 miles from any settlement. Also, you could only find water in a few places. The outlaws knew where the water was and most of the lawmen didn't. This allowed many a crook to get away because the lawman who tried to follow without knowing where to find water would end up with his horse dropping dead from thirst and he would likely have ended up just like the horse.

The people's distrust of the Federal Government due to their past experiences, helped protect many an outlaw. If a fellow was at odds with the Federal Government, the people felt he must be right. If he treated the local people and the church right, what difference did it make what the Federal Government thought of him? So the people including the local lawmen often would not cooperate with the Federal Marshals. My father used to tell me the story of an outlaw by the name of Bill who took advantage of the time and place to make an illegal profit running whiskey to Ute Indians on the White Rock Reservation. At that time, the Indians could not legally buy or use alcohol. So, it was not unusual for the whiskey runner, when caught, to spend long years in prison for this act. They were a lot like today's drug dealers who attempt to make a quick buck by getting people addicted. This destroys many lives.

Bill ran a little frontier outpost, called Dragon, on the Colorado and Utah border, which was beside the Green river. The river supplied irrigation water for fields, beast, and man. Dragon consisted of several low dirt roofed log cabins that housed a store, hotel and bar; all owned by Bill. Also, there was a bunkhouse, ice house, saddle and harness storage, as well as a warehouse for supplies to be kept for the store, hotel and bar.

Much to the dismay of the Indian Agents and the Federal Marshals, Bill's system of smuggling whiskey made the whiskey run about as fast and as full as the mighty Green River. They picked the whiskey up along with other supplies at the railhead at Loma Colorado. They then loaded the whiskey into a freight wagon driven by a jerk line muleskinner who always pulled the wagon with a hitch.

A team was two horses harnessed side by side. A hitch had anywhere from two to ten teams. The first team was hitched to the wagon. Then the driver placed the next team directly in front of the first team and hitched them to the first team. This continued until you had as many teams hitched up in a straight line as you were going to use. The driver or skinner as they called them would ride the left hand wheel horse or mule if they used more than two teams. If less, he would sit on the wagon. To steer more than two teams, they would use a jerk line. This was a long strip of leather about one and a half inches wide, suspended from each team by a strap on a ring until it reached the lead team, which had a short strap connecting them. The jerk line had a Y strap that went to the outside bridle reins of each lead animal. The skinner would give a jerk one way for the lead mule or a different jerk for the off mule. The skinner carried a long whip braided out of raw hide, which would be long enough to reach the lead teams' heads. They always took great pride in their ability to use this whip. They could cut a draft animal to shreds or they could just kill a fly on the lead team with the whip without even touching a hair. They hooked a long chain to the rear of the head wagon and to the front of another wagon so the same teams could pull both wagons. It looked like a double bottom eighteen wheel truck you see going down the interstate.

After loading the wagons, the freighter had to make a long hard 90 mile trip over Douglas pass to reach his destination at Rangley,

Colorado. Depending on the weather, the trip took from five days to two weeks, but they shut down the pass from late October to mid May due to snow. Upon arriving at Rangley, the freighter transferred his shipment on to Bill's hitch and Bill would take it on the final 40 miles to Dragon, where he hid it in his warehouse until he felt safe to make a trip to the reservation to sell the "fire water" to the Utes.

This process went on for many years despite concentrated efforts by the Indian Agents and the Federal Marshals to break the whiskey ring. None of the local people would trust them enough to help. Finally the Marshals decided to send in an undercover agent to try to infiltrate the whiskey ring. It took this agent three years of living and working in the area before anyone trusted him enough to hire him as a freighter on the Loma to Rangely line. However, they didn't trust him enough to tell him what he was shipping.

After getting well out on the trail where no one would be watching him, the agent stopped the team and took a look at his cargo. Over half the load was whiskey so the agent now knew he was closing in on the whiskey runners. However, he still didn't know who was actually selling the whiskey to the Indians because at the end of the line it would be legal for a store or bar to have the whiskey. The agent knew he would have to make his delivery and wait to see who picked up the shipment.

After making the shipment, the agent waited outside town where he could watch who came and went. It took several months as different shipments came in before he figured out that Bill always came to town to pick up groceries right after the whiskey arrived. The agent then contacted the Federal Marshals, telling them that he was sure Bill was the whiskey runner.

Because they did not know who all was involved or whether those that were not involved would side with Bill, the Marshals decided to wait to grab Bill and the rest of his gang after they were well out of town. The Marshal's plan was to halt the wagons and make the arrest. It seemed like a good plan. These lawmen had even made provisions just in case the outlaws did not show any respect for the badge or bullet and broke through the blockade. They placed two other lawmen four miles down the road. They could jump on their horses and chase the bootleggers right into their trap just as you would catch a wild horse by making the poor beast think he was getting away, but instead you were pointing him in the direction of a box canyon where you could trap the mustang. There is some high-

Wiskey for the Utes. "Ole Bill was the smugler that never got caught."

folluting saying about the plans of mice and men that I reckon describe the success of those lawmen's plans, but what does an old cowboy know about fancy words? I do know that those lawmen didn't do a good job of sizing up the guts of the little woman driver or the meanness of Bill and the rest of the gang.

Bill had a sister named Mary who never liked what Bill was doing but never did anything to stop him. She did the cooking and cleaning for Bill. That was not all, she was part of the ring because she went along when the gang went to pick up supplies, driving a four hitch team. She could handle a team better than most men.

Not suspecting that anything might be wrong, Bill, Mary and the rest of the gang arrived at Rangely late in the evening with two wagons each pulled by a hitch with two teams. After they fed, watered and stabled the teams, they went to the hotel to eat. Before going to bed, they quietly loaded the wagons with the contraband whiskey so they would be ready to go well before sun up the next morning.

Things were going very well as the wagons headed down the road in the crisp freshness of the cool morning as the sun began to ascend over the dark form of the mountains. As the sun got higher in the sky, the warmth it gave made everyone feel calm and relaxed. They had been on the road for several hours and were making good time. They had made quite a few miles, when they ran into some unwanted company blocking the road. They were looking into the barrel of four Winchester rifles, with a Federal Marshal attached to the other end.

These bootleggers were not about to let four men on foot stop them even if they were carrying rifles. Bill and the others lead the way in the first wagon. Mary followed in the other wagon. At the sight of the lawmen, the driver of the lead wagon and Mary laid the lash down across the backs of the horses. The tough little mustangs lunged wildly into their collars and were off at breakneck speed. Just as fast, the men in the wagon drew their guns and bullets began to fly. The outburst cleared the road. The lawmens' only chance to stop them here was to shoot the horses. They got the lead team on the first wagon, which caused the second team on this hitch to stumble and fall. The wagon ran on top of the horses causing it to wreck. Quickly, Mary pulled along side the first wagon, slowing just enough for the people in the first wagon to jump on while the cracking of pistol and rifle held the Marshals at bay. Then, Mary lit into her team with the speed of a windmill. Bill, and the rest of the gang were shooting as well as unloading the wagon supplies in the trail to slow the Marshals down. Not that the Marshal cared that much since they knew their trap lay ahead.

When the wagon reached the next blockade, the Marshals met with the same response of flying bullets. These two Marshals were young and inexperienced. Instead of shooting the horses, they shot Mary. As she fell backward into the wagon bed, the team of half-broken mustangs, feeling the lines go loose, put on a burst of speed, which lasted until they dropped in the harness many miles from where their driver was shot. The lawmen, though mounted on faster horses could not over take the gang, because as soon as they were in shooting distance, Bill and his gang shot back. They knew their team would run until it dropped, but that would be long after the Marshals' horses had.

Without whiskey, Bill was ruined financially. Eventually, he turned to sheep ranching where he went broke because of the Colorado and Utah sheep wars. My father always felt bad about Mary. He said she was a good woman caught in a bad situation. You see, no matter how good we are, the wrong type of friend can ruin our lives. Make wise decisions. Do not let others influence you to make bad choices. You must stand on your own.

SHEEP WARS

"No sheep in Rio Blanco County, it's for cattle."

We think of wars as armies lining up and shooting each other. We think of Desert Storm with all the Smart bombs. We think of Vietnam and all the missing men. Before I was born there was a war over sheep. As a child, I listened to the stories from those involved in the Sheep Wars.

The sheepmen hated all predator animals, whether the animals bothered them or not. They shot, poisoned, and trapped animals such as coyotes, wolves, mountain lions and Eagles.

As the sheep grazed on the land, they would utterly denude the land. They ate all the grass and all the weeds. The sheepmen just let them do this until soon there was nothing left to protect the land from erosion. If there was a hard rain, the soil would wash away, and soon the ranges began to wear out. Finally, the government set up the National Forest Service and Bureau of Land Management, and they stopped over grazing.

"Poor lad just wandered across the line."

When the Government told the cattlemen to let sheep come from Utah to the high mountains ranges of Colorado, the determined cattlemen refused to cooperate. The sheep herders were supposed to have a 3-5 mile wide driveway right up the White River. It was about 40 miles to the mountains. It would not have hurt the cattlemen to oblige, but the cattlemen's association was strong.

There were those who beat up sheep herders, hanging them by the neck to a tree. There were those that clubbed sheep to death. They built fences, defied the Federal Government and burned sheep wagons. There were terrible atrocities that accompanied the Sheep War because the sheepmen would not take care of the land.

I remember the story of the poor little boy that wandered 300 feet over the state line or at least that's where they found him with his sheepwagon. They left the boy hanging by his neck in a tree, just because he mistakenly went over the Colorado border. Also, they clubbed the sheep, and killed his horse and dogs.

When the sheepmen came to the county line, they found the roads closed by the county commissioners. Armed men were waiting to ensure the sheep would not get through. They did whatever was necessary to carry out their mission.

My father's cousin, Bill, along with eight Federal Marshals, was able to get his 2,000 head of sheep to the summer range in Colorado. It was only 15 miles to the summer range, but they had to trail them 150 miles out of their way to a railhead and haul them about 300 miles to get around the cattlemen. It took two weeks instead of one day to get the sheep to the summer range. Forest Rangers and Federal Marshals stayed in Bill's camp that summer to protect the sheep.

Finally the cattlemen agreed to let the sheepmen on the land. Bill had won the war. The final range war ended in 1928.

As a cowboy, I never particularly liked sheep. I herded and took care of sheep for my father, but always thought they were dumb. It was all part of ranch country, sheep, cattle and horses.

It made me sad when I listened to men whom I knew personally who in their old age, laugh about hanging some "dumb" sheepherder. If the cattlemen would have respected the law instead of taking the law in to their own hands, they could have reached a peaceful solution. Instead, they were determined to have their own way regardless of the consequences. The result was that many innocent people lost their lives just because they were trying to do their jobs. The cattlemen had a legitimate argument about the destruction done to the land by the sheepherders, but it does not excuse their actions. Eventually, they reached a peaceful solution that allowed the cattle and sheep to co-exist without hurting the land.

If we obey the law and treat people right, things will work out. Today, so many people try to solve their problems with violence and rioting, instead of solving their problems in a peaceful way. This results in many innocent people getting hurt just as it did in the Sheep War. We need to learn the lesson of the Sheep Wars and learn to work out disputes in a peaceful manner.

THE HORSE IN THE KITCHEN

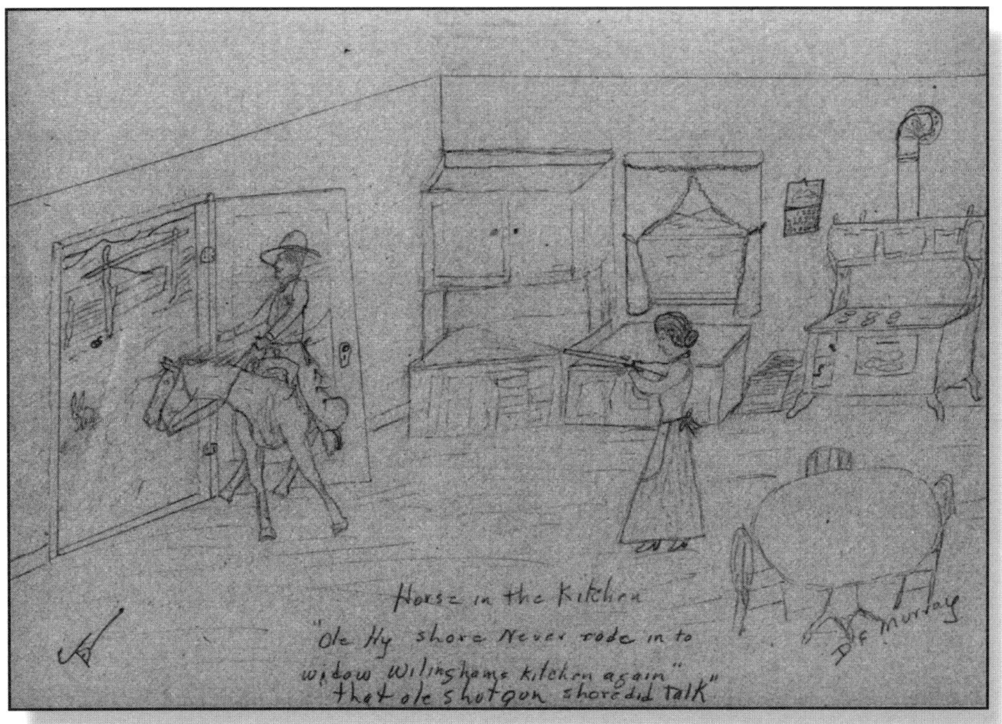

"Ole Hy shore never rode in to widow Wilinghams kitchen again." "That ole shotgun shore did talk."

Hy Bernard worked as ranch manager for Ora Haley's Two Bars Cattle Company. He was a very good manager. Two Bars ran more cattle than any other outfit in the territory, with as many as 160,000 head at times. Their cattle grazed in an area as large as 150 miles square. They had over 1,000 horses in their remuda. The area where the horses grazed was about 30 miles from the main ranch. At the grazing area, they had a large set of pole corrals and bunkhouses for men to sleep.

About half way between the two ranches, stood the old army post called Lay, which was on the north edge of the Ute reservation. The Army established the post about the time of the Ute Indian uprising and named it after the commanding Officer. At the time our story takes place, the Indians were on a reservation in Utah.

When the army vacated the post, the civilians that had worked for the army stayed behind and turned Lay into a town. It contained a few log buildings including a Hotel ran by a lady by the name of Willingham. Her husband had been the telegrapher for the army. About the time the army left, he died. Having no where to go, The Widow Willingham started a hotel in one of the old army buildings to provide for herself because she felt it was wrong to accept any charity. She was known far and wide as a very neat and clean person. Her clothes and hair were always immaculately kept. The hotel reflected this attitude of cleanliness, especially in the kitchen. Everyone respected this lady, so they always washed their faces, combed their hair and dusted off the best they could before entering the dining room.

One day, "Ole" Hy and some of his cowboys had been in town drinking and as a joke one of the men suggested that someone should ride a horse into the Widow's kitchen. Well, "Ole" Hy thought he was just the one to do it since he thought all the ladies loved him, but the Widow informed him that this was not the case, as far as she was concerned. One of the cowboys held the door open so Hy could ride in. He had to lie close to the horse's neck to get through the door. As his horse entered the kitchen, the clicking noise of the horse's hooves on the clean kitchen floor brought the widow with her double-barreled shotgun. As she came through the door, she fired one barrel at "Ole" Hy. Hy and that "Ole" pony left a lot quicker than they had entered and as they turned she emptied the other barrel in that "ole" pony's tail. That pony took off so hard he left Hy sitting in the dust on the ground just outside the kitchen door. He heard the Widow slip another shell into the chamber so he ran for the brush as hard as he could go because he didn't need any more buckshot. As he hid in the brush, he was trying to figure out how to get safely away because every time he would start to leave she would blast away. Finally, after crawling flat on his belly for hundreds of feet he was out of range, his horse was brought to him and he rode away.

Lay was on the only road between the ranch and the remuda. So every time Hy had to go back and forth he had no choice but to go through Lay. Whenever the widow saw Hy, that old shotgun gave him a loud welcome. Many times, a cowboy from one of the ranches would have to come and rescue Hy from the sagebrush where she had him pinned down, and this only ended when Hy left the country.

THE CATTLEMAN

"Ole Con shore had a way with slick calves, to get em to follow him home."

Conwell was his last name, but I don't recall his first name. Everybody just called him "Old Con." I only remember that he was an old man. He was a man that did just enough to get by. Like many people today, Con wanted something for nothing. He had a big family and a little ranch with a few old skinny cows. He worked just enough to keep the family from starving.

As the story goes, he always sold a lot more calves than he had cows. The way this was possible is that Con would ride through the country, looking for calves that didn't have a brand on them. When he found one, he would do one of two things. If the calf was old enough to wean, he would put his brand on the critter and turn it loose to run on the open range until roundup or he would rope the smaller calves and drag them home. Then he fed them milk from a bucket until they were old enough to wean. Once weaned, he branded them and turned them out on the range to grow with the other calves.

A person's brand was the way in which he identified which livestock belonged to him. This was necessary on the open range to be able to distinguish who was the rightful owner of each animal.

The cowboys hog tied the animal to the ground, which means that they tied all four legs together. They built a fire in which they placed the branding irons until they turned red from the heat. They stuck the hot iron on the animal's hide, which burned the hair and hide. This left a scar that was in the shape of the design. This was the brand.

Cowboys made a branding iron by shaping iron into the shape of the person's brand. They registered this with the state brand office. If a person wanted to steal an animal with no brand, he would place his own brand on it or a thief could change a brand by heating a metal rod in a fire, and then shaping it free handed to alter the registered brand.

There was a herd of cattle passing through the country made up of cows and calves. When night came, they were not very far from Con's place. The cowboys left the herd for the night and rode to town to spend the night in a hotel. When Con saw them ride away, he decided he was going to take a look at the herd before dark. In doing so, he found many calves without brands. He did not take any until it got dark. When it got dark, he went back and took about a dozen head of unbranded calves.

As Con drug the calves home, they bawled for their "mammies". He was so busy he didn't pay attention to what those "mammies" were doing. Con shut the calves in the barn and went to bed. A thief

Makin a Count. "Ole Bill could make a good count." "He was a big man, but rode a little horse." "The beef was headin to market."

always gets caught when he is not careful about details.

Early the next morning the drovers came back to start the day's drive. As they were passing Con's ranch, they could hear cows bawling. They took a look at the bawling cows and saw that they were carrying their brand. A short investigation soon found the calves in the barn wanting out, so they opened the door and the calves ran to their "mammies" for breakfast. While the cowboys watched, one of the men went to the door, woke the family and then explained to Con what a good rope could do to a cattle thief.

It was interesting after the explanation how quickly Con got a job and became an honest person. If we practice honesty and hard work, God will always provide for our needs.

HAULING RAILROAD TIES

"Uncle Henry would go to sleep." "Gidup Dan and Jim."

Even though I was just a little boy, I will never forget going to Aunt Laurie's and Uncle Henry's house. They weren't really relation, but that's what everybody called them.

Aunt Laurie had a voice that carried and one could hear her talking half a mile away. She was always busy, making beds, cleaning house and cooking food. It was not unusual for her to have 20 to 30 people around her table at mealtime. The hungry were always fed. If someone needed a place to sleep, Aunt Laurie always found them a bed. There were always people at her house. When I went to Aunt Laurie's and Uncle Henry's house, I always knew I would make new friends.

Uncle Henry and Aunt Laurie came to our valley because of a challenge given by a minister in their church. The challenge was to leave their home and go start another church in a town where there was none. "Why don't you go out and start missions."

So Uncle Henry and Aunt Laurie got on the train and went to the end of the railroad line, which was in our valley. The valley looked promising because it had many new ranches and farms. Uncle Henry staked out a homestead and this is where they still lived when I knew them.

When they first moved to our valley, Henry made his living working for the railroad, hauling railroad ties. He had a good gentle team of horses and a wagon. He got up very early in the morning and headed to the camp were they cut railroad ties. The camp was 20 miles from home. Henry slept most of the way because his gentle team knew the way.

After they loaded the ties on the wagon, he started back down the valley to the end of the railroad. Uncle Henry sat on his load of railroad ties with a sack of hay under him for comfort and he would go to sleep. Many times the team got too close to the edge of the road and a wheel dropped off the edge, causing the wagon to get stuck. Uncle Henry would get down from the wagon, put his shoulder to the wheel and say "gid up Dan and Jim." That team put their shoulders to the collar and with Henry pushing, they pulled the wagon back on the road. Other than occasionally getting off the edge, the team of horses would just plod down the road, pulling the wagon to town while Uncle Henry slept. On his way back he met the other teams coming with their first load.

When they got to town, they pulled up to the railroad siding where the men unloaded the ties. Uncle Henry woke up and the men unload his ties. Aunt Laurie knew the time he got back to unload so she walked the mile to town to bring him his lunch. After eating his lunch, he went back to the railroad tie camp for his second load.

By getting up early, Uncle Henry got three loads a day while the other men got only two loads. The other men stayed up late at night, which made them too tired to get out early in the morning. After they unloaded the third load, he went home, fed his team and slept until early morning, when he began his day again.

On Friday he would only haul two loads, but on Sunday he hauled three loads. He did not work on Saturday. People asked him, “Why don’t you work on Saturday?” In his quiet, gentle way he explained to them and showed them from the Bible why he believed Saturday was “the day of rest.” Whether they agreed with him or not, everyone respected Uncle Henry for his beliefs. He was a man that never compromised his beliefs. Henry never preached to people, but let his actions serve as his sermons even though he was always happy to talk about Jesus if someone asked. In this way Henry raised a church of about 100 members.

Uncle Henry built many of the roads in the county that are still in use today. He took a plow pulled by horses and made the first trail, which they then graded into a road by horse drawn scrapers. Uncle Henry always tried to be of service to the community. He served as county commissioner along with many other public offices.

Uncle Henry requested that when he died, his funeral be held in the church he started. However when he died, the church wasn’t big enough to hold the crowd of over 2,000 people who came to pay their respect for Uncle Henry so they moved it to the biggest hall in town, which still wasn’t large enough. Therefore they brought the casket out in the street and the preacher stood in the door way of the hall so everyone could hear him preach the funeral.

THREE'S A CROWD

"Perry shot ole 'Cookie' down in cold blood."

In our valley there was a lady by the name of Mae who took advantage of men. When a lonely cowboy or farm hand came to town on pay day, she would pick one out and act as if she was in love with him. She would get them to buy her things and take her places until they spent their whole pay check on her. While most of these many men realized what she was doing, this story is about two men that fell in love with Mae.

Old Perry was a farm hand that worked on a ranch near town. He did things like help with haying, milking cows and irrigating. In his younger days, Perry had been a good prize fighter. However, he had taken many a blow to the head, which damaged his mind. However, he was still smart enough to understand the facts of life and wanted to marry Mae because he loved her.

Cookie was a good old cowhand that worked out in the back hills on a ranch. He didn't get to see many men, let alone a woman that would treat him special. So when he came to town, he found Mae's attention much to his liking and he hoped to marry her.

One day, Cookie got paid and took a day off to go to town to see Mae. As he opened the gate of the fence that went around Mae's yard, Old Perry who was already paying a visit to Mae, stepped out of the door and cut down on Cookie with a 30/30 rifle. The bullet hit Cookie and he went down, but he wasn't dead. He pulled his six-shooter and returned fire hitting Perry. Before help could arrive, Cookie bled to death. Although severely injured, Perry held on until they got him to the hospital, where the doctors were able to save him.

The community was irate at Mae over the incident. It was her deception that caused these two men to get into the gun fight. Mae realized this fact as well, and set out to change her life. She went to the hospital and married Perry right on the spot. Then she got religion and became a preacher. Many times it takes a tragedy in our lives before we realize the consequences of our evil ways and are willing to change our lives for the better.

BRINGING HOME THE BEEF

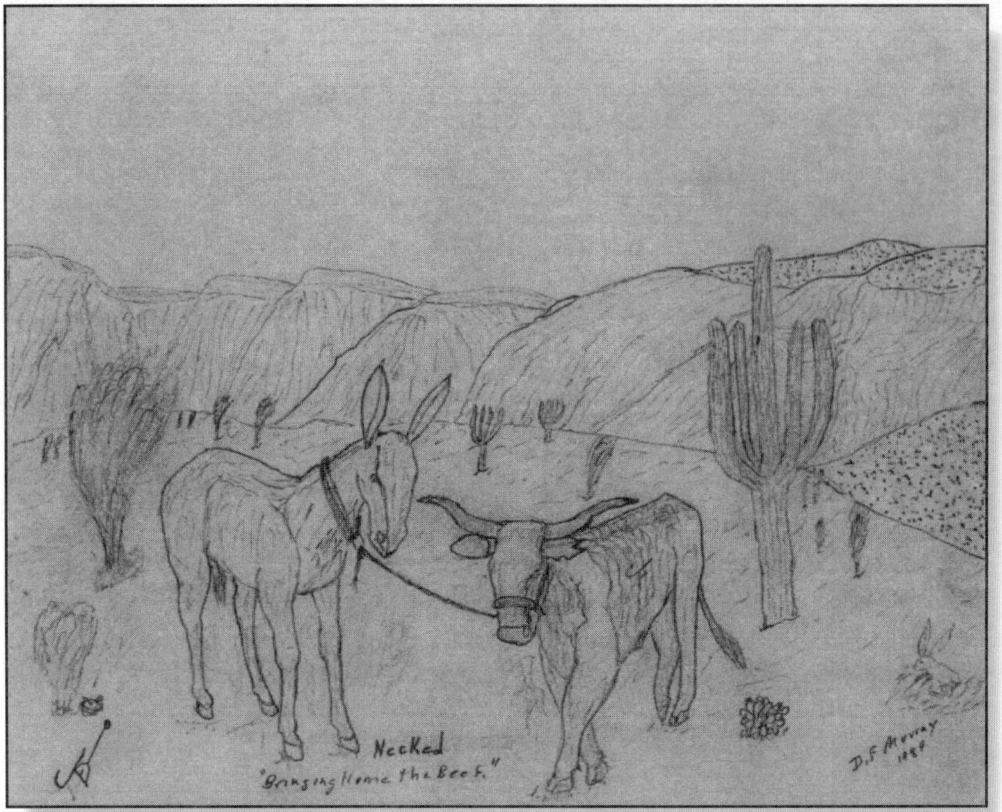

Necked. "Bringing Home the Beef."

There were wild cattle in Western Colorado who were very ferocious if you cornered them. Sometimes cowboys would get together and go out into the hills and chase these wild cows. It might be a bull, a steer or a cow.

They would then rope the cow by the hind feet and head. Then they would stretch the cow out between two horses. The horses would stand braced with their feet back, holding the cow tight. The cowboy took an axe or saw to cut or break the end of the cow's horns off. Then a cowboy led a donkey from the home ranch up beside the cow, haltered the cow and tied it to the donkey.

Sometimes the donkey would be only half as big as the cow, but that really didn't matter because when turned loose, the cow's horns would be too sore to fight, but it wanted to run so it would pull, but the little donkey would just brace its feet, and the cow couldn't pull him around.

The donkey always leaned toward home since that was where he got fed. Maybe it was only one step at a time, sometimes not even a full step. When the donkey ate or drank the cow would have to eat or drink at the same time. The little donkey just kept leaning toward home until in 2 or 3 days they would be back at the ranch and the cow would be broke to lead.

The persistence of those little donkeys tells us a lot. They always had one thing in mind, which was to do their job. We should be like these donkeys. We should set our goals and keep working our hardest to achieve these goals. It might be difficult and we may have set backs, but if we remain persistent, we will succeed.

MULE DEER

"They were shore fat and slick." "That herd ate with cattle all winter."

Western Colorado has the largest herd of mule deer anywhere in the world. One spring when I was a small boy, my father and I saw a doe around our ranch. Along the middle of June, she had a baby fawn who had a deformed right hind foot that made it run in a funny manner.

Across the river from our ranch, was another ranch owned by a man named Dave. He always grained his livestock just as my father did as they wanted them fat and healthy. The old doe was not a bit afraid and when the river was low, she and the fawn would cross and go up to Dave's place, eating out of his feed bunk because she liked the corn. She would eat out of my father's feed bunk as well.

One day my father and Dave caught the fawn and neutered him as you would a kitten or a dog. The fawn grew to be a great big deer. He had the most beautiful set of antlers, but when he ran you could always tell it was him by the way he ran.

Dave and my father always felt the fawn belonged to them. Dave would talk about "his deer" and Father would talk about "his deer" because he would go back and forth across the river between their ranches, but the deer was wild and neither one really owned him.

The years went by and the deer was probably close to 10 years old. He weighed around 600 pounds, which is huge for a deer. He had the most beautiful set of antlers any one had seen because he never fought with other deer. He was gentle and you could get within a few feet of him.

There was a man in town who said that he was going to kill that deer. He couldn't hunt on either place because both were posted. One day he came down the river in a canoe and seeing the deer, he shot at it. The deer hid so the man thought he had killed him. The man went back to town with his canoe.

The next day, he went to find the deer. He found him, but he hadn't killed him the day before. So he shot at him again and this time wounded him. There was an island out in the river and the water around it was very swift and treacherous. There was no way to land a canoe. This island is where the wounded deer went and in the open where everybody could see him, the old deer lay down and died.

You know, there are people that if something's alive they want to kill it instead of appreciating and enjoying it. The man just wanted to kill the old deer. The old time rancher would throw a little extra hay to the deer or elk in the winter time, letting them eat with his cattle. You know many times you can understand how kind and how good a person is by the way he treats his animals.

THE 5TH OF JULY

"Ole Guy had one to many." "Dad needed one more."

While my father was running wild horses on Blue Mountain, he got hooked up with a couple of cowboys; brothers named Guy and Pat McNurlen. Pat's specialty was breaking wild horses. He could stick like glue to a wild horse. The McNurlens had a sixth sense about horses. When they went to chase a band of mustangs they seemed to know where the horses were going, which allowed them to catch many horses. They took my father under their wing and taught him all their tricks.

On the 4th of July when Dad was 16, Guy decided that they had to go to town to celebrate and pick up supplies before leaving. Now the old time cowboy was not a drunkard the way television portrays. On special occasions, a cowboy would buy a bottle of whiskey and get "roaringly drunk," as they called it, as a way of releasing all of their spent up energy due to the lonely life they lived. They would stay in town wandering up and down the streets looking for some fun.

On the Fourth of July, there was usually a rodeo that they would either participate in or watch, along with horse races, running races and contests of all sorts. This particular 4th of July, Guy announced that because Dad was doing the work of a man, it was time he learned to drink like a man. Well, when they got to town, they headed straight for the bar. Guy bought a bottle of whiskey and began to show Dad how to drink. It was not long until they were rip roaring drunk. The next morning, they were still tipping the bottle as they left town. Guy got so drunk that just about daylight, he passed out and fell off his horse. Guy was out cold. Well, the alcohol put an idea in Dad's head. He tied Guy's feet and hands together. He then threw a jacket over Guy's head, hobbled the string of pack horses and headed back to town for some more fun.

It was the middle of the day before someone came along with a team and wagon and found Guy lying in the road trying to get loose, which wasn't good news for Dad. The man in the wagon cut the now sober Guy loose. Guy jumped to his feet, swearing about that no good so and so kid and promising what he was going to do to Dad when he found him. Guy swung on his horse and took off for town like a charging bull.

While Dad was continuing his party, the cowboys kept a look out for Guy since Dad had told them what he had done. When they saw Guy come charging into town, they took Dad and hid him. Dad had to stay in hiding for two days before the cowboys got Guy to calm down by convincing Guy that it was his own fault for getting the boy drunk. With the alcohol and anger out of their system, Guy and Dad were able to return to their work on Blue Mountain.

When we allow anything whether it be alcohol, drugs or our emotions to cloud our judgment, we can get ourselves in all kinds of trouble. We do things that we would not normally do, which can harm those around us as well as ourselves. Who knows what may have happened if the cowboy's had not hidden Dad from Guy. You need to keep a clear head so that you can make wise decisions. If you don't, you might find yourself in a worse situation than Guy found himself when he regained consciousness on the morning of the 5th of July and how Dad found himself when Guy caught up to him.

FAMILY FIGHT

"That ole woman shore went to work on ole Guy with that broom, she sez 'it's a family fight'."

The country was changing faster than the old-time cowboy could comprehend. The U.S. government had opened the finest cattle grazing country to homesteading and the plow, which turned it into some of the world's poorest farm land. Ole Guy felt bewildered by what he saw happening around the country.

One day, while traveling along, he passed a dirt roofed homesteader's cabin. A man was in front of the house sitting on top of a woman, beating her in the face with his fists. From time to time the homesteader would get up and kick the women in the ribs. Because the old-time cowboy had such respect for women, it was more than "Ole" Guy could take. He spurred his horse at a fast run so that he could rescue the lady.

"Ole" Guy pulled the bully away from the woman and began working him over. Things were going well for Guy, when all of a sudden a broom hit him on the side of the head. This surprised him so he said to the woman swinging the broom, "Why are you doing this? I am helping you!" She replied by whacking him repeatedly with the broom. Ole Guy decided it was time to haul freight. As he was riding away on his horse, the woman screamed, "This is a family fight, keep out of it!"

When I see people trying to get mixed up in other people's business, I always think of this story. Maybe as she put it, "This is a family fight." God tells us that where ever possible, live peacefully with all men.

THE LAST GREAT BUFFALO HUNT

"He just stood there." "Them coal miners were shore pouring the lead to him."

Dave Knight was an old Indian that owned a large piece of land in northwest Colorado. He brought some buffalo in and allowed people to hunt the buffalo. It reached the point that the hunters killed all the buffalo except for some old bulls.

There was one of these old buffalo bulls that swam across the river, got on the highway and just stood in the middle of the road. He was a huge old animal and by standing in the middle of the road, cars couldn't get around and many times there would be a line of

Bringing Home the Meat. "That was the last free buffalo." "Dad and Ralph hauled them home."

cars just waiting for him to move. Sometimes people tried to get him off the road by shouting at him or trying to spook him, but he wouldn't leave until he was ready. Sometimes a driver would get tired of waiting and would try to go around and that old buffalo would just bump the car and shove it off the road. There were times a big truck would come along, blowing his air horn and pull up close to the bull and the bull would butt the truck a little, but eventually give up and leave.

Finally, the state highway department told old Dave that he had to get rid of this buffalo. At the Highway department's request, my father and his friend Ralph killed the old buffalo that got on the highway along with one other, but a third one took off as soon as he heard the shots and no one saw him for a few weeks.

It was about three weeks later that a rancher that lived about 25 miles from where they killed the two old buffaloes, heard someone yelling, hollering and shouting. It was during hunting season and this rancher was also the game warden so he went down to see what all the hooting and hollering were about.

As he drove up, there stood the buffalo bull, pawing the ground and snorting. Three drunk coal miners were dancing around this old bull and laughing as they shot bullets into him with 22 pistols and a rifle. They were lucky that when they first started shooting at him, he didn't get angry because he could have stomped them to death. The game warden saw that the old bull was wounded, so he took his big 30/30 rifle and shot him between the eyes.

These men were so proud that they went home bragging. However the next day, the sheriff arrested them for illegal hunting, and killing another man's buffalo. They had to pay for the buffalo, but they didn't get any of the meat.

Sometimes we do things that sound kind of fun or look like fun, but when reality comes the next day, the fun is over. We are responsible for our actions, so you need to think about the consequences of your actions before you act.

THE LAST OF THE GYPSIES

"They were old and very poor."

As a child, I remember seeing the true gypsies, the small, dark looking people with their turbans, fancy little wagons, their old bony horses for travelling and fancy horses for trading. They told fortunes, danced, traded horses and sometimes stole or begged.

Father and I would come along with a team and wagon and a gypsy man would jump out of his wagon, run around and grab our horses' mouth to look at the teeth to see how old it was. All Father would do is say, "Don't touch my horses; they are not for trade." The gypsy would stop and come back, lean against the wagon wheel and catch up on what had happened during the winter.

You see they would travel to the desert in Utah to spend the winter where it was warmer than the high mountains and valleys of Colorado. On the way, they traded horses and would buy horses. If you needed a horse, you looked for the gypsy trader. The people in our valley would tell their children to stay away from the gypsies because they will steal little babies. I wasn't afraid of the gypsies because Father wasn't.

As time went by, the gypsies got jobs and cars. They moved to the city. Finally one fall, only one wagon came through the valley. He was going down to the lower country or to the desert when he stopped to visit with us.

That way of life disappeared because the young gypsies had all left for the city. His wife had died leaving the old man all alone. His old horses were bony and poor. We were in our pickup on our way home when we saw him. We stopped to visit. He shook Father's hand and they had a cordial visit.

Father was a very cordial man. He took in the homeless and hungry, giving them a bed to sleep in and a good meal to fill them up. When we got home, Father got to thinking about the old man and soon he got up and left. I found out later that Father gave the old man twenty dollars. Also, he took the old gypsy some food as well as hay and oats for his old bony horse.

Father and Mother took in the poor and hungry. Nobody ever came to our house, but what they got food, maybe it was just bread and milk or biscuits and gravy, but they always had plenty to eat. We were always giving food away. We always had a bed for somebody to sleep in during the hard times of the depression.

You know maybe a person doesn't go to church, like my father, but Father practiced many Christian beliefs because inside he reverenced "his Maker," as he called God. It is a person's character that matters most. You must always look to be kind and help your fellow man.

I think of the old gypsy as a way of life in the past. The old cowboys' way of life no longer exists. There are young people that think they are cowboys, but that way is no more. As we see life change with the airplanes flying overhead, and the super highways with cars going 65 miles an hour, I think of the slow pace of the horse at 4 miles an hour. My mind goes back to the old gypsies and the old cowboys with their packstrings, herds of cattle and cow ponies. I sometimes look back in sorrow because those days will never be again. This is one of the reasons I wrote this book.

THE END OF THE TRAIL

As my father brings you to the end of his trail, I ask that you stay in the saddle and let me take you for one more short little literary ride. This ride forever changed my life as a result of my father and a big buckskin pinto horse named Skipper.

My father did an exceptional job of breaking Skipper as a cow horse. He could use Skipper as a rope horse or as a cutting horse to sort the cattle. However there was one big problem between Skipper and my father. Skipper thought it was his duty to keep Father humble. Every now and then just as Father put his foot in the stirrup and started to swing on, Skipper would shoot straight up in air, spin a quarter of a turn, land stiff legged with the force of a pile driver and just as quick jump and spin in the opposite direction. This took place in a small area because Skipper never tried to run or get away. He did his bucking in one place, using his energy to twist, turn and attempt to jar Dad loose. Skipper continued to buck as violently as any bronc I have ever seen until he sent Dad flying in an unflattering manner. Skipper always cheated a little because he blew up before Dad got settled in the saddle. Skipper was a big tall horse and Dad has short legs so it was hard for him to quickly get in the saddle. Skipper never bucked if Dad was square in the saddle. Once Dad was on, Skipper worked beautifully. You couldn't ask for a more gentle dependable horse.

The summer after Dad first broke Skipper to the saddle, It appeared that Skipper no longer felt it his duty to keep Dad humble because he hadn't bucked all spring. One day Dad and I moved our cows from one pasture to another. I rode Dusty, our gentle "Ole" cowpony. Dad rode Skipper. The cows didn't particularly want to go so we had worked the horses quite hard. After getting the cows in the pasture, we needed to check the fences to make sure they were up. I talked Dad into letting me get on Skipper. I got off Dusty and dropped her reins while Dad held Skipper so I could get on without him blowing up. I swung on as quickly as I could as I didn't want Skipper to put me at a disadvantage. I got on fine, but as soon as Dad let go of the bridle, Skipper went to bucking. For some reason, Skipper didn't buck as he did with Dad. Instead he took off running and bucking in a straight line, which is easy to ride. Things happened so fast I didn't have time to get scared. Skipper kept going for probably a quarter of a mile. Every time I began to slip, I would hear Dad yelling, "Hold on! Pull his head up! Just as he was about to run in to the fence on the far end of the pasture, he came sliding to a stop. Seconds later, Dad arrived on Dusty who was ringing wet with sweat because she ran so hard trying to catch us. All Dad said was, "Good job son." I turned Skipper and he walked off like the gentlest horse in the world. He never bucked again with me or any other person with the exception of my father who Skipper occasionally gave another lesson in humility.

I have never felt prouder than at the moment my father told me, "Good job son." For in that moment, I caught a glimpse of my grandfather catching wild horses and of my father getting up before daylight to bring in the saddle horses to start the day at cowcamp. That day I learned to appreciate my heritage, not just of my family, but of my country as well. I saw the frontier spirit that made the United States a great nation.

It was my father's desire in writing this book to share this frontier spirit with the readers, to let you glimpse this spirit as I did the day I first rode Skipper. I hope that we fulfilled my father's desire. Whether you are a cowboy from Colorado, a farmer from Nebraska, a fisherman from Maine, a Boston banker or a Philadelphia lawyer we all share in the frontier spirit or I should say the American spirit for it is this spirit that defines us as a united people. It is the American Culture.

There are those today who say that we do not have shared values since our ancestors all came from different countries and different ethnic backgrounds. They say we are a country of all these different little groups that can't get along because we are so different. I disagree with this philosophy, but feel that it may come true if we do not take the time to learn what brought us together as a nation.

Whether they came for adventure, to escape oppressive governments or against their will in the bottom of a slave ship, the people that made America shared certain values. First of all, they were rugged individualists, which means more than wanting to do as you please. To me, Rugged Individualism means to strive to better your life through your own hard work and effort. It means to take responsibility for your actions; to accept the bad as well as the good. It is the determination to not give up even when the situation seems hopeless. It is this determination that settled a wilderness, created wealth previously unknown in the history of mankind and placed a man on the moon.

These achievements became possible because they tempered Rugged Individualism with the moral guidance and discipline proved by their faith in God and the shelter of a strong family. The success of this nation is a testament to the virtue of these values. Do not be influenced by those who attempt to discredit these values. It is our prayer that you will adopt these values in your life. With this prayer our trail comes to an end.

Joe Murray